Cherishing Life

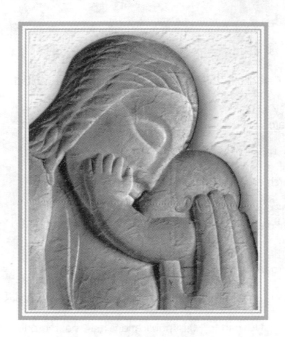

Catholic Bishops' Conference of England & Wales

Cherishing Life

Catholic Bishops' Conference of England and Wales

Published by The Catholic Truth Society and Colloquium (CaTEW) Ltd.

Colloquium (CaTEW) Ltd.
39 Eccleston Square
London
SW1V 1BX
ccs@cbcew.org.uk
www.catholicchurch.org.uk

The Catholic Truth Society
40-46 Harleyford Road
London
SE11 5AY
www.cts-online.org.uk

ISBN 1 86082 256 8

Designed and typeset in L Frutiger Light and Garamond by Primavera Quantrill of the Catholic Communications Service. Cover designed by Stephen Campbell and the Catholic Truth Society. Printed by Stanley L. Hunt Printers Limited.

This publication is available in audio and large print.

contents

numbers in brackets refer to paragraph numbers

3

foreword

In our society, there are many signs of the ways in which human life is cherished; respect for those who live with disability, debate about adequate healthcare for the elderly and widespread concern for the protection of children from harm. The majority of people wish to live in a society where the values of honesty, trust and integrity enable us to flourish as individuals and with others. Such values require the building of an ethos of life that protects persons from womb to tomb, especially the most vulnerable.

However, we can also identify signs of a culture of death; the tragic number of abortions, the demand for legislation which permits euthanasia, diminishing respect for the elderly and the vulnerable, and lack of protection for marriage and the family. There is deep concern about crime in local communities and many live in fear of violence.

Eight years ago the Bishops of England and Wales published *The Common Good and the Catholic Church's Social Teaching*. In that document we addressed then questions of social life in England and Wales as we sought to educate and support Catholics in their social responsibilities as citizens and to help build a society founded on values that are consistent with the Gospel of Jesus Christ. We now present *Cherishing Life* to complement *The Common Good* and to underline our concern to place the gift of life at the heart of all moral reflection and action.

During 1995 Pope John Paul II wrote his encyclical letter *The Gospel of Life (Evangelium Vitae)*. He described the drama between the culture of life and the culture of death enacted in the midst of contemporary societies. In *Cherishing Life* we consider the signs of this drama in our own society and seek to respond in the light of the Gospel and the tradition of the Church.

Jesus Christ calls all Christians to holiness and to make a faithful response to God's gracious invitation of merciful love. Christian faith is expressed through love, good actions and sacrifice - and so every decision involves some renunciation. That is why Christians live in the hope that earthly death is not the end of life, but the beginning of a transformed life shared with the Risen Christ. In *Cherishing Life* we are reaching out to offer this hope to others.

For Catholics, the Bishops give guidance about the teaching of the Church and educate the conscience in the forming of a judgement about what is morally right to do and what is to be avoided. The rapidly developing areas of genetics, medicine and legislation, for example, raise many moral questions and affect everyone living in our countries. As teachers we wish to give guidance about the foundations of the Christian moral life and provide principles to help us all to make a further contribution to public debate: we have an important part to play in society in influencing legislation and shaping values.

We share many values with other Christians and those of other faiths and none and together we can strive to ensure that life is cherished. We hope that in articulating what Catholics believe we can help others to understand the teaching of the Catholic Church and with those who share our values make an important contribution to the common good of our society.

✠ Cormac Cardinal Murphy O'Connor
President
Catholic Bishops' Conference of England and Wales

introduction

In October (1996) the Catholic Bishops of England and Wales published *The Common Good*, calling attention to the social implications of living the Christian Faith. We wanted to help Catholics and other Christians to understand the principles underlying the social teaching of the Church and at the same time to promote human social flourishing for all members of our society.

Our present document, *Cherishing Life*, is complimentary to *The Common Good* and attempts to give a Catholic perspective on some fundamental moral issues relating to the moral and spiritual well-being of the human person in society, especially those issues touching the value and protection of human life.

> *I have come that you may have life, and have it to the full (John 10:10)*

We principally address members of the Catholic tradition in our countries, but hope that others may wish to engage with our teaching. We draw on the tradition, which has informed Catholic teaching down the centuries, as we seek to promote human moral well-being.

We have sought to present our teaching in positive terms, although from time to time we have been critical of opposed views or identified other positions that we judge to be morally unacceptable.

The document is divided into three parts. The first seeks to lay the foundations for moral reflection. We describe some of the more important circumstances that condition our lives. As the human person as moral agent is central to any consideration of morality, we explore the meaning of moral truth and the role of conscience. Moving towards the more particular scope of our document, we finish part one by attempting to answer two questions: 'when does life begin?' and 'when does life end?'

In part two, which we have entitled *Living Truthfully*, we have adapted the well known text of Micah (6:8) to consider a range of particular issues under three general headings: *Walking Humbly*, *Loving Tenderly* and *Acting Justly*.

As a person walks humbly they search for inner meaning or integration, seeking to foster self-respect and looking for a dignified human way of living.

Loving tenderly leads us into a consideration of the principal elements of the Church's tradition about love, friendship and sexuality. Men and women are called to a life of love lived in a way that is unfettered by self-seeking or exploitation of the other. Such a life has a number of different forms and requires norms and boundaries which give it direction and protection. In this section we address ourselves particularly to issues touching marriage and family, irreplaceable reference points for any treatment of love and sexuality.

Seeking to protect the dignity of every human being and to promote their flourishing, we consider in acting justly a number of issues that, in justice, must be promoted to secure the appropriate treatment of human beings in relationship to each other. In particular we explore some of the complex issues of bioethics and face up to the more obvious threats to human life.

Our third and final section concludes the document by outlining the specific responsibilities of society, individual citizens and the Church in working to build a culture of life that puts human moral welfare and the cherishing of life in all its stages in prime position.

It is our hope that this document will help readers to understand why the teaching of the Church is as it is, and will enable Catholics in particular to develop a moral approach to the many new issues that confront us, especially those arising from the rapid expansion of medical science and technology.

part one
foundations

1. In the words of the Gospel, Jesus came so that people 'may have life and have it to the full' (*John* 10:10). The word 'life' is rich with meaning. The many different species of plant and animal each live and flourish in ways appropriate to their kind. All have life, but the life of a tree is not like the life of a bird, and the life of an insect is not like the life of a warm-blooded animal. Among this vast variety, human beings have a unique kind of life with the possibility of understanding themselves and living responsibly. The life promised by Jesus is a share in the life of God; this is life in its fullest and deepest sense. It will be experienced to the full in the world to come, but begins already under the inspiration of the Holy Spirit as Christian faith, hope and the love of God.

2. When we talk of 'cherishing life', we have in mind life in all its senses. Our use of the word 'life' will shift between the various levels of meaning: biological, human, moral and divine. This is deliberate, as consideration of matters of life and death should not be abstracted from the profound significance of being human. To cherish life is to care for living people: it is a matter of what or who we care about and what draws us to care. We will focus on issues that touch in different ways on the meaning of human bodily life and the way in which people's lives need to be cherished, for example: the place of marriage in society, the use of advance directives, and the possibility of cloning and gene therapy. Issues such as these are widely debated in contemporary society and are of concern to many people. We wish to proclaim a positive message of hope and support for all those working for the protection and enrichment of human life and to offer principles to help approach difficult situations.

3. Catholic Christians discover how to value every human life not only through reflection on Scripture, on the example of the saints and on the teachings of the Church, but also by the use of their reason and understanding, and through the experience of seeking to live out the Christian life in the contemporary world. Thus, to cherish life in our world and in our society, it is necessary to be aware of the situation we are living in. We start, therefore, by paying attention to the joys, hopes and fears of people's lives. These are 'signs of the times' which Christians interpret in the light of the Gospel. They help to give the context for reflection on what needs to be done and on how we can cherish life in practical ways.

signs of the times

health and medicine

4. Over the last fifty years our countries have seen huge improvements in the standard of living. Measured in purely physical and practical ways, living standards continue to rise. Life expectancy has also increased significantly. New advances in medicine are announced almost daily and operations are now routinely performed which would have been unthinkable only a few years ago. Research on the human genome and on stem cells seems to offer hope of a cure for many diseases that are currently untreatable.

5. However, technological advances can have negative as well as positive effects. While ultrasound and other advances in technology have given us beautiful images of the child in the womb, this seems to have had little effect on the protection our society is willing to extend to the unborn. In principle, termination of pregnancy is only permitted in restricted circumstances but, in practice, the number of abortions has reached epidemic proportions: over 186,000 in 2001 (Office of National Statistics). At the same time, thousands of human embryos conceived during fertility treatment are abandoned and some of these are even used for experimentation.

6. Those who are seriously ill or dependent can face the twin fears of unwanted and aggressive overtreatment, or of discrimination, being deprived of proper care or treatment, being regarded as 'bed blocking'. Use of advance directives is being promoted by government, while the courts have condoned passive euthanasia, that is the intentional taking of life by withholding or withdrawing treatment or tube feeding, especially in the case of patients in a persistently unconscious state. In contrast to this, many physicians and general practitioners are better trained in palliative care, and the hospice movement continues to attract a great deal of public support. In this movement we see a sign of real hope.

7. As people live longer (life expectancy for men and women is five years longer than it was in 1976 according to the Office of National Statistics) the relative age of the population is increasing. Older people are rightly  concerned about the collapse of home care services and other services once provided by local authorities. They fear rejection and isolation. Not everyone enjoys safe housing and some face real concerns about high levels of street crime or burglary. It is unclear how the nation's pensions will be paid for in the future. There are also real anxieties about rationing in healthcare. Who will suffer most from shortages of doctors, nurses, hospital beds, and other essential resources? Employers, hospitals and governments sometimes discriminate unfairly against older people. However, attitudes towards older people are changing and people now have more opportunities in their later years than any previous generation.

8. Attitudes towards people with disabilities are also shifting. Institutions including businesses, colleges, churches and community centres have begun to question how they can become more accessible to a diverse range of people, especially to those with special needs. These changes have been supported by new laws and reflect a greater recognition in society of the abilities people possess and can share with others once their practical needs have been adequately addressed. While these moves are very positive the same cannot be said of the prevailing approach to prenatal diagnosis and screening. Since 1990 it has become legal to terminate pregnancy for reason of disability at any time up until birth. This is an invidious form of discrimination which runs completely counter to the positive steps being taken to acknowledge the equality of people with disabilities.

marriage and family

9. Marriage and the family are fundamental institutions within our society. There remains a great desire for the stability and support possible in marriage. Every year hundreds of thousands of people get married, intending to share their lives with one another. Weddings are celebrated as times of great joy and hope. The love that parents show to their children is the gift that makes society possible. Despite pressures of work, many parents make great efforts to spend as much time as they can with their children and, working closely with their schools, seek to educate them in what is most worthwhile and valuable in life.

10. However, changes in our society have had a significant effect on the institutions of marriage and the family. Relationship breakdown, divorce, and alternative partnerships are accepted by many as part and parcel of modern life. For instance, in 2000, while there were 305,000 marriages there were over 154,000 divorces (Office of National Statistics). This has had a devastating effect on the bringing up of children, as separation and divorce commonly leave children hurt and confused.

11. Witnessing so many marriages break down, some couples no longer see the value of going through a marriage ceremony and prefer simply to live together. Couples in this situation have begun to argue that the law should give them the same status as married couples. Parliament has sought to reflect this change in society by voting to amend the law on adoption so that an unmarried couple could adopt as a couple. However, it should be noted that, at present, the rate of relationship breakdown in cohabiting unmarried couples is significantly higher than is the case in married couples.

12. Threats to family stability can arise from various external factors, for example, poor housing, unemployment and low income. Violence and crime can make neighbourhoods hostile to family life. As a parent, it is hard to combat the power of television and magazines, the advertising that is directed at children, and the influence of their peer group. Much of children's media is creative and responsible, but many parents are concerned at some of the messages that come from these sources. It sometimes seems to be assumed that, to be normal, a teenager should be sexually active. Also troubling is the encouragement of fashion and self-consciousness about body-image even in young children, and the unrealistic presentation and glamourisation of wealth and celebrity.

society

13. In *The Common Good* we noted the place of politics in public life and stressed the importance of people bringing their faith and goodwill to the political scene. However, many still lack confidence in politics and do not accept that they have a substantial responsibility to take part in elections. At 59%, the turnout at the 2001 general election was the lowest since universal suffrage. Such widespread disillusionment with the whole political process, especially among the younger generation, is a cause for concern.

14. Not only governments, but all public institutions have suffered from a crisis of credibility. Doctors, nurses, social workers, clergy, teachers and the police have lost the standing they once had in the eyes of the public. Many are viewed as being paternalistic, exclusive or discriminatory. Increasingly, professional bodies are suspected of covering up the truth about events and always protecting their own. In turn, this mistrust has undermined morale and made professionals more defensive.

15. Another recent trend is the growing tendency to believe that whenever there is an accident or whenever a mistake is made then there must be someone to blame. Solicitors *increasing litigation* are now allowed to advertise their services *has major and* on a 'no win no fee' basis and people are *worrying* encouraged to sue for damages. However, *implications for* we should remember that not every tragedy *many institutions* is blameworthy. Moreover, the great multiplication of expensive inquiries and court cases could itself become a threat to the common good.

Increasing litigation has major and worrying implications for many public institutions, not least the financing of the National Health Service. It was estimated that in 2002 the NHS was facing negligence claims totalling £5.25 billion (UK National Audit Office).

the world

16. In 1995 in his letter on issues relating to life, *The Gospel of Life (Evangelium Vitae)*, Pope John Paul II called on Christians and men and women of goodwill to help build a culture in which life is cherished. He saw several signs of hope for this in modern attitudes. He mentions 'a new sensitivity ever more opposed to war' and 'a growing public opposition to the death penalty' (paragraph 27). In this country, the new sensitivity spoken of by the Pope has shown itself especially in opposition to waging a war except as a last resort and when it has a clear legal and international mandate.

17. Concern to protect the lives of the most vulnerable in the poorest countries of the world has led to various valuable initiatives by individuals, governments and international bodies. The Jubilee 2000 campaign was remarkably successful in persuading governments and world financial institutions to take steps towards releasing the poorest countries from their crippling debts. Another encouraging sign is the greater public awareness of the need for fair international trade in order to promote balanced development in the poorer countries, and to help foster world peace (see our extended statement *Trade and Solidarity*, 2003, issued together with the Bishops' Conference of Scotland in association with CAFOD and SCIAF). And yet, despite the great efforts that have been made, a combination of war, the power of affluent countries to determine trade relations, political and commercial corruption and environmental destruction has sometimes led to a state of deprivation that leaves whole populations vulnerable to famine. Adding to these problems, one of the greatest threats to human life across the world and especially in Africa is posed by the

AIDS pandemic from which 3 million people died in 2001. Worldwide, there are an estimated 42 million people currently living with HIV or AIDS (World Health Organisation estimate).

18. There are many international relief and development agencies working for justice, development and the environment throughout the world, such as the Catholic agencies CAFOD and Caritas - social action. Their work receives a great deal of support from the general public and this in turn promotes important values of solidarity within our society. However, while much good work is done, not all development projects are equally worthwhile. In particular, it seems that certain international agencies, under the guise of promoting reproductive health, have risked becoming instruments of injustice. For example, China's infamous one-child policy has been linked not only to coercive sterilisation and abortion, but also to the selective abortion, infanticide or neglect of girls. In 2000, the United Nations estimated that some 60 million girls who would be expected to be alive were 'missing' from various populations, particularly in Asia (UNFPA State of the World Population 2000). There have been persistent allegations, hotly denied, that programmes funded through the United Nations have been complicit in such abuses. (See for example Standing Committee D on the International Development Bill, Proceedings 22 November 2001)

19. Food is more plentiful, readily available, varied, and safer than in previous generations. In this country most people have plenty to eat. However, even here many health problems are related to diet and it is still the poor who suffer most in this regard. The crises over BSE and foot-and-mouth disease have exposed questions about the way in which our food is produced. The development of GM foods is only the latest of a series of controversies about responsible and safe use of technology in agriculture.

20. The poorest countries of the world are blighted by preventable disease and premature death because of poverty and inadequate nutrition, hygiene and sanitation, which are themselves partly caused by a history of global and local injustice. Reports such as the Acheson

Report on Inequalities in Health in 1998 have shown that, even within a wealthy country such as the United Kingdom, ill health is closely related to relative poverty. There are also several specific groups within our society who are particularly vulnerable: those who are homeless or who are addicted to drugs or alcohol, those who have come to the United Kingdom seeking asylum, older people who live alone, and those who are severely disabled.

advertising constantly feeds the illusion that what we buy can bring us happiness

21. An effect of greater wealth in the West is that we have become a consumer society. Advertising constantly feeds the illusion that what we buy can bring us happiness. Many are left struggling with debts they cannot hope to repay. Some seek pleasure to escape from the world, while others try out of curiosity what then becomes an addiction. Pleasure-seeking and addiction are as old as the human race, but drug abuse seems to be an increasing problem for our society, particularly among children. According to statistics published by the Department of Health, in 1998 11% of children aged 11-15 admitted having taken illegal drugs in the previous 12 months, by 2001 this figure had risen to 20%.

the church

22. Christian reflection must take into account not only the concerns of the wider world but also the situation within the Church and people's attitudes towards the Church. The Catholic Church has undergone great changes since the Second Vatican Council (1962-1965). Catholics are now encouraged to work and pray alongside Christians from other traditions, to become involved in dialogue with people of other religions and to engage in the common struggle for justice. Many Catholics have become involved in these activities and been inspired by the vision put forward by the Second Vatican Council.

23. At the same time the period since the 1960s has been a painful one for many in the Church. To some the implementation of the Council seemed to go too far, to others it did not go far enough. The great social changes in the family and society have also had an impact on the Church and the crisis of trust that has affected the public professions has also affected the clergy. In recent years, confidence in the Church has been damaged by the way it failed to deal adequately with the scandalous abuse of children by certain individual priests and religious. While the Church has subsequently sought to address this issue, for the victims of the abuse the damage has already been done.

24. In response to the challenges facing the Church and the world many Christians together with others have committed themselves to work in the service of life. In some cases this has been through their professional lives in education, social services or healthcare, in other cases, through voluntary work in these and other fields. At the same time, Christians have spoken out on social issues in defence of the vulnerable: refugees and the homeless, those who are ill, people with disabilities, the dying and the unborn.

25. The life of many parishes has been invigorated by individuals and families who have given their time to building up the local Church as an open and effective community. Catholic schools continue to be a major feature of the life of the Church and work hard to create inclusive and distinctive communities known not only for results or good discipline, but also as places of life, hope and tolerance, even though some people outside and even inside the Church perceive Church schools as symbols of division.

26. Many of the issues we have mentioned as 'signs of the times' involve matters of international justice. These are matters of great concern that will not be absent from our discussions, but they also demand special attention in their own right. This applies in particular to the phenomenon of globalisation, whether that is seen as a beneficent trend or as a threat. Therefore, in parallel to this document, we are preparing a project on *The Global Common Good*. These two aspects of justice should not be thought of in isolation from one another, nor in isolation from the considerations set out in *The Common Good*, but in relation to one another. Concern about international justice and concern about the protection of innocent life should go hand in hand.

27. Our situation in the present day with regard to health and medicine, marriage and family, the state of society, of the world and of the Church gives us a context for moral reflection on human life. This is the world we live in and within which we have to act. However, to act morally we also have to have a sense of direction, of what it is we are trying to achieve. Before looking at some specific issues, it is appropriate to consider more deeply what it is to act morally, and also to reflect on the limits of human life: when it begins and when it ends.

acting morally

moral truths

28. Many different religions and philosophies recognise the fundamental human need and responsibility to pursue what is good and to live according to what is true. There are good or valuable aspects to life that are acknowledged by virtually everyone: friendship, peace, rewarding labour, knowledge and understanding, health in mind and body, integrity of character. On the other hand, we know all too well that there are also actions and attitudes that disfigure the human character: fear, prejudice, greed, envy, love of violence and abuse of power.

29. These features of human life bear witness to our common humanity. There is an equality and an inherent dignity shared by all human beings and this is the basis of an objective moral order and of universal human rights. The Second Vatican Council and recent popes have developed and defended a Christian account of human rights and of corresponding responsibilities founded on the dignity of the human person. The Catholic Bishops' Conference of England and Wales has also addressed this matter in its reflection: *Human Rights and the Catholic Church* (1998).

30. The Golden Rule 'do to others as you would have them do to you' (*Matthew* 7:12) bears witness to a principle recognised by all people of goodwill: do nothing unjust or unfair to someone else. The scope of the moral law goes beyond avoiding harm to others. It is also necessary to show positive human solidarity with others in various ways, for instance, by supporting communal projects especially for the needy, by paying tax, by showing courtesy to those we meet and love and gratitude within our families. Solidarity is also expressed in important ways through that network of relationships below the level of the state and outside the immediate family: relationships with friends, workmates, neighbours, colleagues, fellow churchgoers, people from the same village, town or region, membership of trade unions and professional bodies, of political, social or sporting organisations. The requirements of the Gospel go further still, demanding that we concern ourselves with the needs of strangers and foreigners and that we love our enemies and pray for them (*Matthew* 5:44).

31. There have been several international attempts to identify a definite list of human rights so that these can be protected. International conventions such as the *Universal Declaration of Human Rights* (1948) and the *European Convention on Human Rights* (1950) seek to defend human life and well-being from unjustified attacks.

personal autonomy is not the only human good

However, the concept of rights used in these documents needs to be examined carefully, for rights imply responsibilities. Personal autonomy is not the only human good, and an adequate theory of rights will place the need for individual freedoms in the context of the common good. This includes for instance, the requirement to support the institutions of marriage and family life as well as the importance of other expressions of human solidarity.

32. Contemporary British society is characterised by a plurality of approaches to moral questions. One influential approach is the utilitarian idea that something is right if it results in the best consequences, as measured by the greatest happiness of the greatest number of people. This might seem reasonable at first sight. However, it can easily lead to discrimination against minorities, especially if happiness is defined simply as what people want or prefer. It is, of course, important, when weighing up possible courses of action, to consider their potential consequences, insofar as we can foresee them. However, the prospect of good consequences cannot justify acts which are morally wrong in themselves. It is always wrong intentionally to torture or kill an innocent person, even if pragmatic considerations might sometimes make such action seem attractive. Moral choices should promote true human flourishing and be fair and just to everyone.

33. Another common attitude to moral questions is to claim that morality is based solely on feelings and is a purely private matter for the individual. Someone might say 'I feel this is right, but it might not

be right for you' or 'I feel this is wrong, but I can't impose my moral views on others'. However, those who use such expressions usually do so inconsistently: for example, if no actions can be said to be wrong, then imposing views on others cannot be said to be wrong. Experience shows that people engage in serious moral arguments precisely because they think that something objective and important is at stake. Furthermore, moral relativism is harmful if it leads people to remain silent in the face of injustice. The wrongness of slavery or torture, rape or child abuse, lies in the objective harm they do as a contradiction of the human good and the moral order.

theological foundations

34. Church teaching on moral matters is founded not only on reason and argument, but also on Scripture and the Christian tradition developed through reflection on Christian practice, and through the teachings of saints, popes and councils, under the guidance of the Holy Spirit. Moral theology uses a method of reasoning enlightened by faith to develop moral arguments. Faith is not incompatible with reason but complements it, and reflection on the mysteries of the faith illuminates and deepens our understanding of human life.

35. A great early Christian writer, St Irenaeus, once wrote 'the glory of God is a human being fully alive, and full life for a human being is the vision of God'. Christians believe that life has meaning, and that the meaning of life is to find happiness through Christ in friendship with God in the service of others. We all have to discover for ourselves where the path to human fulfilment lies: this will differ from person to person and is found in relation to persons: as needing and as needed by others. Each person has a unique life to lead; a call from God to his or her own destiny with and for others.

36. Jesus showed that the one God is three persons, Father, Son and Spirit. Each is God, all are one, living in relationships of eternal love. From this mystery we draw truth for our own relationships. Treating people morally and respectfully involves recognising them as persons. The question then arises, who qualifies as a person? This is similar to the question a lawyer once asked Jesus, 'who is my neighbour?' (*Luke* 10:29). Jesus replied with the story of the Good Samaritan who cared for an injured man who had been attacked and robbed. The Samaritan, even though he was a foreigner, recognised the need of a fellow human being. The parable urges that the term 'neighbour' be used in a wide and inclusive sense and not restricted so as to exclude anyone. In the same way, all human beings, whatever group or class they belong to, should be recognised as human persons with basic human rights.

Christians believe that life has a meaning, and that the meaning of life is to find happiness through Christ

37. The Scriptures warn us of the reality of sin in ourselves and in others. The story of Cain and Abel (*Genesis* 4:1-16) tells how envy fractures the peace intended by God and leads to domestic strife, violence and murder. However, since Jesus came to seek and save the lost (*Luke* 19:10), the recognition of sin in the life of the Christian is not a reason for despair. Rather it is an invitation to repent and trust in the mercy of God granted through humble confession and reconciliation. The path to holiness is a step by step growth through conversion, often through many falls and many new beginnings.

38. The resurrection of Jesus from the dead shows that death is not the end of the human story. The life of the body is not an absolute good, but it should be cherished both for itself and as the opportunity to serve and to be with our fellow pilgrims. Because this mortal life is a gift from God, it is reserved to God to bring it to an end, to bring us to judgement and then, please God, to grant us eternal life. It is necessary to surrender our lives to God, both in living for God and in accepting death from God's hand when the time comes. Jesus spoke of the need to die in order to find life (*John* 12:24-25), and this refers both to the Christian life here on earth and to the promise of life in the world to come. Thus the attitude of the martyrs was not to seek death but to accept death readily when it was necessary, out of love for Christ and in the hope of being united with him. This is the meaning of Paul's words 'to me, living is Christ and dying is gain' (*Philippians* 1:21).

39. God creates each human being to be the centre of a new world that is his or her story, a whole world in miniature, a microcosm. In this sense every human being is irreplaceable. The dignity of each human being is founded on his or her creation in the image and likeness of God (*Genesis* 1:26-27). The divine image is shown most perfectly in Jesus, the Son of God, who came

every human being is irreplaceable and invaluable

in human form to restore human beings to a right relationship with God and with one another. The image of God is thus seen more clearly in love and humility than in power and worldly honour. As a gift of the Creator, human dignity can never be earned or withdrawn, but flows from the very fact of human existence. It transcends differences in ethnic, religious and cultural heritage and is possessed equally in common by each member of the human family.

40. As every human being is irreplaceable and invaluable, it is always wrong intentionally to kill an innocent man, woman or child. This conclusion is also implied by the commandment 'You shall not kill' (*Exodus* 20:13). Nevertheless, we should note that the scriptural

commandment does not apply to all killing. It does not forbid the killing of non-human animals, as is clear from the laws on the ritual slaughter of bulls and goats. Furthermore, sometimes even the killing of people is presented in the Scriptures as excusable or as legitimate: for instance, unintended killing in self-defence and killing in a just war. The teaching of the New Testament affects how Christians read the Hebrew Bible, but the New Testament also contains passages that appear to justify the use of the sword (for example, *Romans* 13:4).

character and conscience

41. 'Make a tree sound and its fruits will be sound; make a tree rotten and its fruits will be rotten' (*Matthew* 12:33). Good actions can only be sustained by a good and reliable character. Character is formed through the many everyday practices, actions and decisions which either draw a person closer to God, to others and to personal integrity, or lead towards alienation from self, others and God. Through good actions we grow in the virtues. For example, practical wisdom helps us make the right choice. A just disposition secures fairness in our relations with others. Temperateness or moderation builds a right attitude to the goods of the world. Courage overcomes fear so that we can act well in the face of danger. Through prayer, the sacraments, and loving action, the Christian grows in faith, hope and the love of God.

42. Growth in virtue involves a deepening sensitivity towards what is right and wrong. It begins with the determination to live rightly and the willingness to learn how to judge wisely. The ability to make considered judgements recognising the moral quality of an action is termed 'conscience'. The judgement of conscience should be a prayerful one, made in consultation with people we can trust, with the aim of conforming to the truth. It should be adequately informed about the moral principles that apply to the act as these determine the moral quality of the act, as well as the circumstances and the intended moral good. In this judgement, a person confirms and takes responsibility for his or her own actions. Conscience is, then, that personal core and sanctuary where an individual stands before God.

43. Moral maturity involves growing in wisdom and in grace within and with the help of a community so as to be able to make the right judgements in particular situations. Christians see this as part of conversion to Christ. It is a life-long task. Education of character and conscience is a gradual process in which the developmental stage of each person needs to be respected. It is first situated in the home, within the family and in the local Church community, including its schools. Here a process begins which continues insofar as each person takes increasing responsibility for his or her own learning. Continuing adult education is important in a world of rapid change and new moral questions; for instance, in the fields of medicine, technology, economics and politics.

44. Conscience may be clouded by cultural perspectives or by honest ignorance, but in such cases the judgement of conscience does not lose its value. If someone has sincerely tried to discover and to follow the truth, but has mistakenly done something wrong, then he or she will not be at fault. Everyone is bound to follow their own best judgements and to take responsibility for their actions. However, recklessness or an unwillingness to find out what is the right thing to do will not excuse a person from blame if his or her bad choices result in wrong actions. Ignorance is not always an excuse.

45. Many factors will influence a person's moral judgement: experience, family, culture, and faith community. Often an individual will be hampered in living truthfully because he or she lacks freedom in particular moral choices. The academic disciplines of psychology, the study of family systems, class analysis and economics can all help illuminate these limits to freedom in relation to the development of personality. Nevertheless, while the effects of trauma or dysfunctional family background cannot be overcome easily, with God's help there can be psychological and spiritual healing and growth.

46. While everyone should seek to avoid doing wrong, sometimes it is impossible to avoid cooperating in the wrongdoing of others. For example, a good citizen should pay tax to contribute to schools, hospitals and upholding law and order, but it is very likely that some of this money will be used in ways that some people would find unconscionable, for instance, in paying for weapons of mass destruction. Catholic moral theology distinguishes two kinds of cooperation, formal and material. Formal cooperation means both actively helping and sharing the evil aims of the other person. This is something a conscientious person should never do. Material cooperation means helping someone accomplish something but without sharing that person's aims. Such cooperation can still be morally wrong, but at times it may be morally justified, for example, when one cannot opt out without jeopardising even more fundamental human goods than the evil tolerated. To return to our example, it is still right in principle to pay taxes even when we know that some of the money will be misspent.

it is right in principle to pay taxes even when we know that some of the money will be misspent

47. The moral assessment of material cooperation is complex. It requires practical wisdom to take full account of the various factors involved and reach a judgement of conscience: Are there alternatives available? How urgent is it to act? What goods and what harms are at stake? How do each of these goods and harms relate to the action? Is there a reasonable likelihood of misleading others and thereby 'giving scandal'? What are the precise circumstances of the situation? How does this action conform with the individual's particular role, responsibilities and vocation? Consider the case of someone who works for a company that supplies medical instruments and who becomes aware that the company has recently started supplying abortion clinics. Having recognised this, one person may be called by God to object to such involvement, even at the risk losing this job, so as to bear prophetic witness to the evil that is being done. Someone else might recognise that abortion is wrong, but legitimately accept this level of cooperation in order faithfully to follow his or her vocation to support a family or for the sake of other worthwhile goals.

the role of the church

48. Interpreting the story of the rich young man, Pope John Paul II described Jesus as a patient and sensitive teacher who leads the young man step by step to the full truth about the meaning of human life (*The Splendour of Truth (Veritatis Splendor)*, 1993, paragraph 8). The bishops, as successors to the apostles, have the role of confirming moral teaching, clarifying the moral approach to new questions and identifying misunderstandings that may cloud moral judgement. In this work bishops are assisted by the scholarship of theologians and other academics, as well as by the wisdom and experience of lay Christians. The teaching role of the bishops, especially when it is exercised collegially by the bishops acting together in union with the pope, is called the Magisterium.

49. The Catholic Church collaborates with others in seeking a deeper consensus about the inviolable dignity of the human person. Ecumenical initiatives such as the report of the Anglican-Roman Catholic International Commission (ARCIC) *Life in Christ* (1994) signal the Church's commitment to seeking, where possible, unity of Christian witness on moral matters.

50. Church teaching guides us to find the truth and to hold on to it with certainty. We recognise that some Catholics have difficulty with certain teachings of the Church. Yet Catholics have a right to receive the fullness of the Church's teaching and they have a corresponding duty to adhere to that teaching (*Catechism of the Catholic Church* 2037). One should not, however, look to the Church to produce concrete answers for every practical question. Priests and bishops 'will not always be so expert as to have a ready answer to every problem (not even every grave problem) that arises; this is not the role of the clergy; it is rather up to laymen to shoulder their responsibility under the guidance of Christian wisdom and with eager attention to the teaching authority of the Church' (*The Church in the Modern World (Gaudium et Spes)*, 1965, paragraph 43). There are many particular decisions, in the sphere of public policy for instance, in which the moral principles taught by the Church leave scope for prudential or practical judgements. Even in these situations the Catholic Christian must seek to ensure that his or her judgements are indeed informed by correct moral principles.

51. The Church as teacher has the task to proclaim moral truth with clarity, but 'she must be careful not to break the bruised reed or quench the dimly burning wick,' (*The Splendour of Truth*, paragraph 95, quoting *Isaiah* 42:3). The moral life is a response to God that may require difficult choices. However, as St Augustine pointed out, 'God does not command the impossible'; what God requires of us is made possible by the working of grace in our weakness (cf. Council of Trent, *Decree on Justification*, c.11). The Church, as a community of disciples, is called to walk with those who struggle in the moral life, offering compassion and understanding to those who fail to discern and to live out God's loving will.

52. In every society, including our present one, conscientious Christians will sometimes find themselves at odds with the accepted moral standards of the time or even with the law of the land. In our society this may happen, for instance, in regard to the recognition of the right to life of children in the womb. People should not be forced to act against their conscience and the law ought to recognise a right of medical staff to refuse to perform actions that they consider to be morally wrong. Nevertheless, often Christians will suffer as a result of holding fast to moral beliefs and may be denied promotion or advancement in a profession. Here the Christian bears witness to the dignity of human life, to the inviolability of the moral order, and to the holiness of God's law. This builds up the local Church and the local Church in turn is called to support the person involved.

conscientious Christians will sometimes find themselves at odds with accepted moral standards of the time

the limits of human life

53. There is a mystery at the heart of each of us that cannot be reduced to our place in society or the talents or qualities we happen to have. Christians express this mystery by saying that every human being has a spiritual 'soul' directly created by God. We should always think of soul and life together as in the phrase 'the life and soul of the party'. The soul is not something extra added to human life, but is what moves and shapes that life.

54. The human being is neither merely a physical body nor merely a ghost living inside a body. The human being is a living whole, a unity of body and soul. This unity is the foundation of many rights, for instance, the right to religious freedom. People need to express their spiritual lives in bodily ways, through actions, words and gestures, as in the words of Scripture 'use your body for the glory of God' (1 *Corinthians* 6:20).

when does life begin?

55. At conception or fertilisation, the fusion of the gametes from each parent produces a new biological individual, a cell with a completely new genetic identity. From the beginning, the embryonic human exists within a network of relationships: as the offspring of a mother and a father and as the gift of God the creator. Each embryo is a living being, possessing the dynamic potential to develop, in interaction with his or her mother, passing through many stages of development first inside the womb and then outside.

56. The qualities we think of as being most distinctively human do not show themselves until much later in life. However, we should not judge things only by how they appear at one particular time; we must also consider what they have in them to become. Babies are human beings before they can walk and talk, even though many of their abilities have not yet become fully apparent. With an embryo we are considering the very earliest stages of human development, but the principle is the same. The humanity of the embryo shows itself as he or she grows and develops. What is hidden and mysterious unfolds and becomes evident with time. The human embryo should therefore be regarded as 'not a potential human being but a human being with potential' (*Abortion and the Right to Life*, 1980, paragraph 12).

57. In many different places and using many different images, the Scriptures bear witness to the involvement of God in the origin of each human being in the womb. God creates our innermost being, knits us together, weaves us in secret (*Psalm* 139:13-16); fashions us like clay, pours us out like milk and curdles us like cheese, clothes us with skin and flesh (*Job* 10:8-11); gives us life and breath, sets in order the elements within us (2 *Maccabees* 7:22); sends breath into the bones in the womb (*Ecclesiastes* 11:5); inspires us with an active soul (*Wisdom* 15:11). The Scriptures show God calling, naming and setting apart those he has chosen even while they are still in the womb: Jacob in the womb of 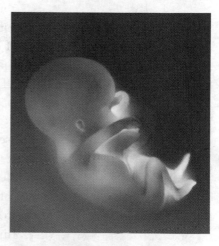 Rebecca, Samuel in the womb of Hannah, John the Baptist in the womb of Elizabeth. When Mary was told that she would conceive and bear the Son of the Most High she went in haste to visit her cousin Elizabeth. There she was greeted as 'the mother of the Lord' (*Luke* 1:43). For nine months, the Lord dwelt in the womb of the virgin Mary.

58. Not only Christians, but many other people believe that God is present and at work within the embryo from the beginning: God knows the one he is fashioning. From the first century, Christians have recognised the human being that God is forming in the womb as sacred and inviolable. While theologians have speculated about the origin and nature of the soul and canon lawyers have debated what penalties are appropriate for abortion, the moral stance of the Church has remained unchanged: any attack on the embryo, however young, has always been regarded as a serious sin against God and against the developing human life.

59. Furthermore, a living being of human parentage and with human potential, whose status as a human person is at least arguable, to put it no more strongly, must be given the benefit of the doubt. For this reason, Pope John Paul II has reiterated the teaching that 'the human being is to be respected and treated as a person from the moment of conception' (*The Gospel of Life*, paragraph 60).

60. Some people cast doubt on the status of the human embryo because, in the normal course of events, many embryos fail to implant and are lost. This reasoning perhaps gains its force from the smallness and thus, on a superficial level, the apparent insignificance of the embryo. However, the logic of the argument is to move from the rate of mortality to the (supposed) lack of intrinsic worth. Once this is made clear, we can see that the move is groundless and the logic is dangerous. For much of history, and in many parts of the world today, infant mortality has also been very high. Nevertheless, we should not regard human life as expendable simply because it is vulnerable. We should do what we can where we can. The existence of spontaneous embryo loss (the true extent of which is in fact uncertain) should not cause us to be unconcerned for human embryos in situations where their fate lies in our hands.

the human being is to be respected and treated as a person from the moment of conception

61. A more perplexing question has been raised about the status of the embryo in relation to identical twins. Occasionally a human embryo will divide within the first few days of development and produce twins. Nevertheless, there is no contradiction here. If one human embryo gives rise to two human embryos, this is an instance of one living being giving rise to two living beings, something not unknown elsewhere in nature. The process of twinning does not contradict the fact that the human embryo is human. The embryonic human is not a disunity or a haphazard collection of cells, but a living, dynamic, self-organising, integrated being. The human embryo is, quite simply, a very young human being. Whether the embryo that gives rise to identical twins is thought of as one, as actually-one-but-potentially-two, or as two, there is never less than one human life present and he, she or they need recognition and protection.

when does life end?

62. Death is the loss of life, the disintegration of the living unity of the human being. Traditionally Christians have described death as the separation of body and soul. In the words of Scripture 'the dust returns to the earth as it once came from it, and the breath to God who gave it' (*Ecclesiastes* 12:7).

63. In ordinary circumstances death is diagnosed on the basis of irreversible loss of breathing and heartbeat. However, when a patient is on a ventilator the diagnosis of death is more difficult. In these circumstances medical authorities in the United Kingdom have accepted brainstem death as the death of the patient on the grounds that it inevitably causes the collapse of the bodily system as a whole. In his *Address to the Transplantation Society* in August 2000, Pope John Paul II accepted as a criterion for ascertaining death 'the complete and irreversible cessation of all brain activity' but only on the understanding that this can be considered 'the sign that the individual organism has lost its integrative capacity.'

64. In 1998 the Department of Health suggested as a definition of death 'the irreversible loss of the capacity for consciousness combined with the irreversible loss of the capacity to breathe'. The government has subsequently asked for comments on this definition. From a philosophical and theological standpoint, this cannot be considered an adequate definition of death. The ability to breathe spontaneously is one feature of a living body, but it is by no means the only such feature. More thought must be given to what constitutes the functioning of a living body and how to determine when 'the individual organism has lost its integrative capacity' (Pope John Paul II, *Address to the Society for Organ Sharing*, 1991). If the body retains its capacity to function as a living whole then it is alive, even if the capacity for consciousness is lost. Someone who is in a coma or who is in a persistent unconscious state, is not actually dead and medical authorities rightly distinguish persistent unconsciousness from biological death. Death must not be redefined so that it includes patients who are alive but who are judged to be 'as good as dead'.

part two
living truthfully

65. In his letters, Paul encourages new followers of Christ to live in a holy way: 'live lives worthy of the calling to which you have been called, with all humility and gentleness, with patience, bearing one another in love' (*Ephesians* 4:1-2). Again he writes: 'whatever is true, whatever is pure, whatever is honourable, whatever is just, whatever is pleasing, whatever is commendable, if there is any excellence, if there is anything worthy of praise, think about these things' (*Philippians* 4:8). It is not difficult to find lists of human virtues in other parts of Scripture or in other inspiring writings. There is more than one way of cataloguing what is involved in living in a genuinely human way, and so, more than one way of structuring a discussion of moral questions.

66. In drawing up this document we drew inspiration from a passage in the book of the Prophet Micah:

> *This is what the Lord asks of you: only this, to act justly, to love tenderly and to walk humbly with your God* (*Micah* 6:8)

67. We find this passage refreshing in its directness and simplicity. It is surely by walking humbly, loving tenderly and acting justly that we will effectively build up a culture in which every human life is cherished. This passage also reminds us that a Christian account of justice should be framed by love and mercy, and that a Christian account of love should begin with the love received in humility from God. In this sense every moral issue could be considered to come under justice, love and humility together. The inner unity of these virtues should be borne in mind as we use this passage to give a threefold scheme for our discussion of particular moral issues relating to life.

walking humbly

searching for meaning

68. There is a restlessness about the human heart, a need to make sense of the world and to discover peace of mind. This desire is common to people throughout the world and finds expression in many different traditions of philosophy, theology, prayer, spiritual exercise and meditation. Some of the spiritual practices of other cultures have started to become popular in this country, especially with people who are disillusioned by their experience of their own religious heritage but who still realise the human need for a spiritual dimension to life.

69. While not every belief or practice is equally valid, and it is wrong to adopt a kind of 'pick and mix' attitude to the spiritual life, the Church welcomes every attempt at serious inner reflection. This is understood by Christians as an expression of the common and fundamental human desire for communion with God. There is within us a spiritual 'homing instinct'. Because we are created in the image and likeness of God, we find ourselves drawn towards God as the One we really wish to be with. In the words of St Augustine, 'you have made us for yourself and our heart is restless until it rests in you.'

70. Everyone, including those who are uneasy with talking about God or with established religion, may 'walk humbly with God'; that is, live with an awareness of being on a journey with the One who is inexpressible. The passage from Micah is an invitation to recognise this as the loving presence and companionship of God throughout life. Faith comes as the realisation that it is not primarily we who search for God but it is God who seeks us out and accompanies us on our journey.

71. Christian faith involves an explicit acknowledgement of God as the source of all life, a firm belief in Jesus as the ultimate revelation of God and a recognition of the Holy Spirit as God at work in the world. The

Christian sees walking humbly with God as following Christ, and sees Christ in all who walk humbly. A committed Christian will naturally want to bring all people to know Jesus and to appreciate what God has done through Jesus' life, death and resurrection. However, the Church rejects nothing that is true and holy in other religions: 'Let Christians, while witnessing to their own faith and way of life, acknowledge, preserve and encourage the spiritual and moral truths found among non-Christians, together with their social life and culture'. (*On the Relation of the Church to Non-Christian Religions*, 1965, paragraph 2)

72. Recognising God as God has moral implications. The acceptance of God's sovereignty provides us with a fundamental orientation, giving colour and direction to all the decisions, actions and practices that make up our lives. The movement of the human heart towards God, and our recognition of life as a gift from God that is rich with meaning, enables us to value our lives and the lives of others.

73. Walking humbly with God implies finding inner integration and developing a spirit which is free from selfish or destructive attitudes. While many violent actions may stem from desperation at the experience of injustice, oppression or economic exploitation, much violence and harm is also the result of untempered passions such as greed, envy, pride, anger or avarice. These destructive desires are in turn the result of discontent or unease in ourselves. Finding rest within ourselves is thus an important part of acting morally and the cherishing of life.

finding rest

74. A primary manifestation of our humble response to God's gift is the way we care for ourselves body, soul and spirit (1 *Thessalonians* 5:23). It is a feature of our society that some people seek fulfilment in destructive ways, for example, the abuse of drugs or sexuality. Such misguided ways of life can result in grave physical, mental and spiritual harm. The problem of self-destructive behaviour can be seen as a spiritual as well as a psychological problem. We need to help one another to appreciate the goodness of life and to hold on to the real possibility of living life well, even in difficult circumstances. Fundamental to this is discovering a proper kind of self-love and self-respect.

75. We need to understand and resist the influences that spread despair and undermine the spontaneous love of life. We, as well as our political representatives, should turn our attention not only to the state of the economy and national security, but to the conditions in which people live. Space, rest and recreation - in the proper meaning of that term - are vital to human well-being. The physical environment in which people live and work, their job security, and the time they have available for nurturing relationships with friends and within the family can either enhance or undermine a culture of life and hope. Hope only flourishes where there is a positive culture to support it.

76. Some people suffer because they are forced to work long hours with little time off so that they feel continually both physically and mentally exhausted. For others work can become a kind of addiction which they find exhilarating, but which becomes both self-destructive and particularly dispiriting for their families. There is a wisdom in the biblical commandment that one particular day of the week be set aside as a common day away from work. Sunday trading regulations aimed to protect a common day of rest for the sake of leisure, family life and spiritual recuperation for everyone. The continual erosion of these laws threatens the existence of any common public rest and is making our society one of ceaseless activity.

Sunday is not only a day of rest and for family life, but also a day for prayer and worship of God

77. For Christians, Sunday is not only a day for rest and for family life, but also a day for prayer and the worship of God. Prayer, both individual and communal, is a natural expression of the human spirit and a central part of every religious faith. It is the pre-eminent source and expression of spiritual well-being.

prayer

78. Prayer is one way we express in our everyday lives our relationship with our Father in heaven (*Matthew* 7:7-11). It is an expression of communion with God, traditionally described as 'the raising of the mind and heart to God'. Prayer is a mutual activity in which God gives himself to people and they give themselves to God. In some ways it is like the mutual self-giving of friends. Prayer may be a shared conversation of asking, thanking and praising or simply talking; it may occur through the activity of meaningful gestures, music and ritual; or it may be a silent communion - wordless, expressionless and depending only on conscious presence.

79. The Judaeo-Christian tradition bears witness that prayer is both a personal and a communal activity. The worship of the community is an important aspect of prayer. As John Donne wrote, 'no man is an island, entire of itself; every man is a piece of the continent, a part of the main'. We belong to a society, and it is in society, beginning with the family, that moral growth takes place, that conscience is formed and that spiritual well-being is fostered. For the Christian the local Church community is a focus of support and guidance, in particular through its public celebration of prayer. This plays a profound part in guiding the individual and the community to an acceptance and understanding of their responsibility towards each other.

80. The Catholic Church enshrines this important human value in her requirement that Catholics participate in Mass on Sunday and certain other major days. Those who have been baptised become members of the body of Christ (1 *Corinthians* 12:12-27) which is the Church. Catholics express this common identity, witness to their faith, and strengthen themselves and one another by sharing in the communal celebration of the Sunday Eucharist, in the cycle of daily prayers, and in the annual cycle of days of special prayer, vigils, fasts and feasts.

81. Prayer and the way we live go hand in hand because, for believers, God is as real as the air we breathe. There is no aspect of living from which God can be excluded. Whatever our choices, whether for good or ill, we draw God into them. If our choices are for good they deepen our relationship with God; if they are for ill they compromise that relationship.

caring for one's health

82. Each of us also has a serious moral obligation to care for our physical and mental health. This obligation does not forbid us to take risks, especially in showing love for other people. It should, however, affect our choice of lifestyle. An approach to life that seeks to wring out of every experience the maximum pleasure for oneself is ultimately self-destructive and debases the rational and spiritual nature of the human person.

83. The quest for personal satisfaction, if it is driven by a 'me first' philosophy, is destructive not only of the individual but also of the community to which we belong. Our instincts and drives should serve the whole person and the community. The abuse of drink or drugs gives rise to a whole range of social evils from fatal road accidents to crime and disruptive behaviour. It can also lead to a person being unable to cope with the responsibilities of money, work and family and so failing to help and support others. The abuse of sexuality has social costs in its effects on the network of relationships with friends and colleagues and its effects on public health. The pleasures of consumerism have dramatic global and environmental consequences of which we are not fully aware. Even the search for health can be destructive if it becomes just another obsession.

84. In a culture that seeks to sell people the latest product by appealing to the immediate pleasure it will bring, it is difficult to achieve a healthy balance in life. We need to cultivate our desires and emotions so that they respond appropriately to attractive and pleasurable things. The measure of what is reasonable is given by what is beneficial for health and for other important human and social goods. If our desires are well ordered, we are not imprisoned, but liberated, both because we flourish as individuals and because we are able to contribute more fully to our communities. The wisdom of this approach is reflected in contemporary interest in preventative and holistic healthcare.

85. Ill-health is a part of our human condition and has a general relationship with our alienation from God and each other. The more immediate causes of human sickness are manifold - poverty, environment, diet, stress, allergic reaction, bacteria or viruses, poisons, genetic factors, ageing and accidental injuries. Some forms of illness, especially mental illness, illnesses brought about by lifestyle, and illnesses associated with death such as AIDS, attract social stigma; it is all too easy to respond to such conditions by denying human community to the person so affected. A better attitude, more firmly based in the Christian tradition, is to see illness in others as requiring a response of love and care, and illness in ourselves as making us aware of our human frailty and our need to live a life based on love and able to accept love from others.

86. Most if not all of us have to contend with illness at some time or other. Illness is an occasion of spiritual need. It provides a challenge to our faith, our hope and our love to remain able to appreciate life even in the midst of suffering. Particularly distressing is the phenomenon of mental illness which may deprive someone of the ability to direct their own lives. People suffering from mental health problems will often isolate themselves, even seeking to end their lives violently. Many people experience depression to differing degrees and some require intense medical treatment in hospital, prolonged psychotherapy, or life-long medication.

87. The wider community has a responsibility to provide people who are ill with adequate and reliable support and access to the help they need. Neither mental or physical illness nor disability can strip people of their dignity as human beings, no matter how severe the condition.

humility and creation

88. An important aspect of human well-being is the relationship we have with the rest of the created world. This is an area where the virtue of humility, of walking humbly with our God, is especially necessary. The word humility comes from 'humus' meaning ground. This reminds us of the story of God creating Adam from the dust of the earth (*Genesis* 2:7). While we human beings tend to pride ourselves on our achievements and on our status as being above other creatures, we should never forget where we came from, and out of what we were made.

we should never forget where we came from, and out of what we were made

89. To flourish as human beings, we need to breathe clear air, drink clean water and eat safe food. We are relatively fortunate in this country to enjoy such gifts although they are sometimes threatened by pollution or disease, but we should not shirk from asking ourselves how far our own well-being may be directly linked to the deprivation of others. In other parts of the world even the basic necessities of life are not easy to secure. Recent investigations have found that the forests of the earth, the stocks of fish in the seas, and the wonderful diversity of animal and plant life on the planet are all at risk. This is due to a considerable extent to over-exploitation and pollution. Furthermore, many scientists are now convinced that high levels of gas emissions from the fuel we burn are changing the climate of the planet. These changes could be devastating, causing disruption of weather systems, rises in sea level and flooding affecting millions of people.

90. In his 1990 *Letter for the World Day of Peace*, Pope John Paul II spoke of the relationship between world conflict, injustice and the 'lack of due respect for nature, by the plundering of natural resources and by a progressive decline in the quality of life.' The goods of creation were given for the benefit of all people, but they are being exploited by and for a minority. The harm that is being done to the planet will affect everyone, but the poor will suffer most as they will be unable to escape the worst effects.

91. Ecological responsibility can begin locally through simplifying our lifestyle, reducing and recycling waste, using public transport or car sharing, and paying close attention to the environmental effects of what we buy. Local and national government have an important role in ensuring the reduction and responsible disposal of domestic and industrial waste, but they need the support and cooperation of the public. Though many Britons now live in big cities, many others live in or very near the countryside. The rural economy should be supported in ways that will secure lasting benefits for those who live and work there, that will enhance the local community, and that will support appropriate means of food production and protect the environment as a gift for all people.

92. Society and the Church face new questions in addressing developments in biotechnology. For example, the question of genetically modified food has become a central issue both within developing countries and within more developed countries. There is concern about the safety of such products, the problem of the irreversibility of genetic modification and the possible impact on other forms of life. In developing countries, a particular concern is to ensure that the poor do not become more vulnerable to the economic system by becoming dependent on the multinational companies who supply these products. Genetic modification raises the question of the limits to interference with nature: when does the human person cease being steward of creation and begin to abuse it? The rapid pace of technological development will make massive demands on our capacity for moral reflection.

93. The presence of BSE in animals and the suffering of people from CJD have raised awareness of the fragility of the relationship between humans, animals and nature. The untrammelled pursuit of profit can lead to methods of farming that fail to ensure the adequate care of animals. Though they should never be seen as equal to human beings, other animal species are God's creatures too and by their very existence they bless God and give him glory. All life comes from God and the world shows God's glory by its richness, its variety and its interrelations. This is the meaning of the biblical phrase 'God saw all he had made, and indeed it was very good' (*Genesis* 1:31).

94. The need to cherish the gift of the environment is a major challenge for the 21st Century. Some of the most important issues in this area are considered in our reflection *The Call of Creation: God's Invitation and the Human Response* (2002). There we emphasised that whereas 'our destructiveness can silence creation's song of praise to God, our care of creation can be a true expression of our praise' (*The Call of Creation*, part IV). This perspective challenges the narrow economistic view that the gifts of creation have no value except as factors in production.

95. A belief in God as creator gives Christians a framework and motivation for reflection on the beauty of creation, and for care and wise use of its goods. *The Canticle of Brother Sun* illustrates St Francis of Assisi's love and respect for the creator and redeemer of nature. For this reason he has been named as patron of those who support ecology. The mystic Hildegard of Bingen also celebrated the fertility of God's earth in her writings. Respect for the environment requires a spiritual foundation and a conversion of heart if we are truly to wean ourselves away from the excessive consumerism of our current lifestyles.

loving tenderly

love and friendship

96. When, in the Gospel of Matthew, Jesus is asked to name the greatest commandment of the Law, he responds by giving not one but two commandments: to love God with all our heart and soul and mind, and to love our neighbour as ourselves (*Matthew* 22:36-40). It is clear therefore that love is the absolute foundation of Christian life and morality. Yet it is true that 'love' is a word that is frequently misunderstood. It is sometimes used as a synonym for sex but this is doubly wrong: for there is sex that is not loving and there is love that is not sexual. Love can take many forms. There is the love between parent and child, the love between brothers or sisters, the love between relatives, the love of home or country. Social friendships and good relations with colleagues are important in life, though we would not usually describe these as love. There is, however, a friendship that is profound and that we can have with only a few people who are very close to us. Here it is possible to talk of love. The love of true friendship may be between members of the same sex or between members of the opposite sex. Friendship of this sort is a great value and is always to be honoured and respected.

> *love is the absolute foundation of Christian life and morality*

97. Love shows itself most characteristically when someone is suffering or in need. The Gospel according to John tells us that Jesus loved Martha, Mary and Lazarus. When he heard that Lazarus had died, Jesus wept. He returned to Judaea and raised Lazarus back to life even though he knew that by doing this he would attract further attention from the authorities and place his own life in great danger (*John* 11:1-53). Jesus called his disciples his friends and taught them that there is no greater love than to lay down your life for your friends (*John* 15:13).

98. In order to love another person it is necessary to have that security that comes from having been loved. This is why the love of parents is so important for a child's personal development and growth. There is a wrong kind of self-love, a selfishness that is both harmful to others and self-destructive, but there is also a right kind of self-love, a self-respect that enables us to love others. It is from our first carers that we learn how to love ourselves and how to love others in the right way. True self-love is not arrogant or greedy but is honest and open hearted.

99. The scriptural phrase 'love tenderly' could also be translated 'love kindness' or 'love steadfast love'. This refers to the steadfast and generous love that God has for human beings and that we all, as human beings, are called to show to one another. Through the Gospel we are set free to love others, knowing that we ourselves are loved by God. 'In this is love, not that we loved God, but that he loved us and sent his son to us' (1 *John* 4:10). Loving tenderly follows walking humbly because we must first be able to accept love if we are truly to love others. Human love is thus both a gift of God and a sign of God's presence. It reflects the way that Father, Son, and Holy Spirit are with and for each other, three persons distinguished and united by mutual and equal relationships. It is for this reason that Scripture says, 'God is love and anyone who lives in love, lives in God' (1 *John* 4:16). As images of this divine reality, our noblest act is to give ourselves to another person in love. As Paul wrote, 'faith, hope and love abide, these three, but the greatest of these is love' (1 *Corinthians* 13:13).

the church's teaching on sexuality

100. The Church draws its teaching on the meaning of the human body from Scripture where the creation of embodied human beings is seen as the peak of the goodness of material creation (*Genesis* 1:26-31). Belief in the goodness of the body, present everywhere in the Jewish Scriptures, was confirmed by the coming of Jesus when 'the Word was made flesh' (*John* 1:14). Christians believe Jesus to be the

Son of God born in Bethlehem as a real, flesh and blood human being, at once fully divine and fully human. Jesus' victory over death took the form of a bodily resurrection, again underlining the significance of the human body. Christians believe that in the life of the world to come they will share in a general resurrection of the body in a transformed world. Moreover, even in this present life, the human body is 'the temple of the Holy Spirit' (1 *Corinthians* 6:19).

101. It is because the human body has value and significance that there can be a positive meaning discerned in the bodily ways we relate to one another. If the body did not matter then it would not matter what we did with our bodies. However, because the body is included in the goodness of creation, the sexual meaning of the body should be seen as a blessing and a proper aspect of human nature. Sexual attraction is an important aspect of human life that therefore needs to be expressed and integrated in a fully human way.

102. What is implied by the fully human expression of sexuality? Popular culture, films, novels and songs, though they often present a distorted or overly-romantic account of sexual love, nevertheless commonly see the meaning of sexual encounter in terms of love. Indeed, in ordinary speech people talk of the 'act of love' or of 'making love'. It is true that this sentiment is contradicted by the equally common tendency to see sexual intercourse as meaning as much or as little as someone wants it to mean. However, to think of the human sexual act as though it could be merely a recreational activity undermines what is most human and most significant about sexual intimacy.

103. Because sexual intercourse has a human meaning, it can be thought of as 'saying something'. There is a language of the body. A couple who are committed to one another in marriage express their love for one another in many ways: in their shared life through actions, words and deeds. When they express their love through sexual intercourse the couple are effectively saying to one another that they love their husband or wife, are committed to that person, have eyes for him or her alone. They are also saying that it is with this other person that they, together, can welcome a child as the fruit and object of their love. That is why it is a betrayal when a husband or wife has sexual intercourse with someone else. People who have experienced sexual betrayal may feel they have been lied to, because what the other person 'said' in the act of love is contradicted by his or her actions.

104. The context for sexual intercourse should be one of genuine, exclusive and committed love. Indeed, the love implied in making love is nothing less than the love that is expressed in marriage. Young people are rightly wary of committing themselves too hastily to the serious reality of marriage. This is the reality entailed by love that is exclusive and unconditional. It is also the context within which the couple can best welcome a child, if one should result from their love. Clearly, it is difficult for many people in our society to take seriously the idea that sexual intercourse should take place only within marriage, but the language of love still points to this as its true context.

the love implied in making love is nothing less than the love that is expressed in marriage

105. In order to be able to integrate our sexual desires with the rest of our personality and with what is important in our lives we need to develop the right disposition. Christians call this disposition the virtue of chastity. This virtue includes sensitivity to a person's situation and to the circumstances in which people find themselves. Where a relationship is possible and appropriate, it is right for a couple to express affection and mutual attraction, and for married couples to express their love through sexual intercourse. On the other hand, if a particular relationship is inappropriate, it is wrong to foster sexual desires towards the person concerned. For married couples, showing sexual affection is a positive virtue and an aspect of their mutual communication. Chastity is a virtue both for those who are married and for those who are single. It means thinking and acting appropriately with friends or with colleagues and, within a relationship, being honest and sensitive without selfishness or thoughtlessness hindering the communication of love. Self-restraint will always be at the service of genuine love and sensitivity.

being single

106. For the majority of people, in the past and in the present, marriage has been, and continues to be, the normative relationship by which men and women live together as a community of life and love. Nevertheless, it is a positive feature of our society that it has also become much more acceptable to live as a single person. This is due to many factors, but not least is the marked increase in the number of unmarried people. People are less likely to marry out of a desire to conform; people are also more wary of the commitment of marriage; they are tending to marry later; many marriages are breaking down; and widows and widowers are living many years after the death of their husband or wife. If we also consider couples who are separated from one another for months or years by adverse circumstances, it becomes clear that living as a single person is now a common state within our society.

107. Some people who are single have made a definite choice to remain single for the freedom this brings or because of demands of work to which they feel committed. Commitment to a particular work or responsibility may also prevent someone from meeting people and developing the relationships that might lead to marriage. What makes such a life sustainable is the network of good relationships with others, and especially the existence of some close friendships. Someone who is single may not be any less happy or gregarious than someone who is married. Indeed, people who are married but who have no relationships outside the

it is in the circumstances of the present that each person is called by God to walk and love and act

marriage that can sustain them (as can happen, for example, if the couple moves to a foreign country) may feel more isolated than are those who are single but who have their friends around them.

108. There are many people who have not made any choice that would rule out marriage but who are as yet unmarried. Perhaps they would welcome marriage, but they have never found the right person.

Perhaps there was someone they wanted to marry but they were not able to. They do not feel especially 'called' to the single state, but this is where they find themselves and thus, this is where they must live and act. All of life is a pilgrimage during which we must attend to the opportunities that lie immediately before us. Situations change, but it is in the circumstances of the present that each person is called by God to walk and love and act. It is in our work and voluntary activities, in church and in our local area, through colleagues, friends, relations and neighbours that we discover our vocation in the present moment. This is equally true for those who are married, for those who are single by choice, and for those who are single for the time being.

109. Those who are married and then widowed face a double trauma. First there is the pain of losing someone who had been such a large part of the person's life. It may be 'better to have loved and lost than never to have loved at all', but it is certainly more painful to love and then to lose. The second trauma is readjusting to the state of being single. This involves both practical and emotional changes. Some may find it difficult ever to think of marrying again. Others do wish to remarry. Many change their views over time. The teaching of the Church is that the wife or husband who has died in Christ is at rest with the Lord, but for the one who remains alive, the earthly pilgrimage continues and he or she is free to marry or to remain unmarried, according to God's call for them. Throughout history those who have lost husbands or wives have played a very significant role using their time and freedom in the service of others and of the Church. This is as true today as in the first days of the Church's existence.

110. Some people are not free or able to marry, though they would like to. Those who remain faithful to marriage vows, even after a painful separation and divorce from their husband or wife, uphold an important value. In their case, the single life is a witness to the sanctity of marriage. Again, for this to be sustained the support of friendship is vital. The development of a more positive account of the single life offers an opportunity for people in this situation to gain a richer understanding of their calling. The call of God is a call to walk humbly, to love tenderly and to act justly wherever we find ourselves.

homosexuality

111. The Church utterly condemns all forms of unjust discrimination, violence, harassment or abuse directed against people who are homosexual. Consequently, the Church teaches that homosexual people 'must be accepted with respect, compassion, and sensitivity' (*Catechism of the Catholic Church* 2358). In so far as the homosexual orientation can lead to sexual activity which excludes openness to the generation of new human life and the essential sexual complementarity of man and woman, it is, in this particular and precise sense only, objectively disordered. However, it must be quite clear that a homosexual orientation must never be considered sinful or evil in itself.

the Church teaches that homosexual people must be accepted with respect, compassion, and sensitivity

112. As marriage is such a fundamental form of human relationship, it is vitally important to establish an adequate understanding of its meaning or purpose. The Church has consistently argued that the meaning of marriage is not set by society alone. The essential meaning of marriage is given in God's plan of creation. In the beginning God created human beings 'male and female' (*Genesis* 1:27). It is from the personal union of man and woman that new life is born and it is within the loving context of such a relationship that a child can be welcomed and nurtured. Marital love involves an essential complementarity of male and female.

113. The Church teaches that sexual intercourse finds its proper place and meaning only in marriage and does not share the assumption common in some circles that every adult person needs to be sexually active. This teaching applies to all, whether married or unmarried, homosexual or heterosexual, engaged, single through choice, widowed or divorced. Everyone needs to develop the virtue of chastity so as to live well in his or her own situation. Moreover, there is more to a person than sexual inclination and more to love than sexual desire. The late

Cardinal Hume emphasised the message of the Gospel that all love is from God and that each person is precious in the eyes of God. 'The love which one person can have for and receive from another is a gift of God' (*A Note Concerning the Teaching of the Catholic Church Concerning Homosexual People*, 1997), paragraph 17). The Church recognises the value of friendship between homosexual people when it is lived chastely in accordance with her moral teaching. What the Church does not countenance is any attempt to express this love in a sexual way.

114. The present state of the law and common public opinion reflect the immemorial belief founded on the natural law that only a relationship between a man and a woman can be a marriage. There may be people who hold this view out of fear or prejudice, but the position is not itself arbitrary or unfair and it should not be regarded as discriminatory. Furthermore, attempting to create a legal category of 'same-sex marriage' threatens to undermine the meaning and status of marriage. Nonetheless, it may be necessary, as many have argued, to remedy by law unjust situations in which the bonds of friendship are improperly disregarded (for instance, being excluded from appropriate consultation regarding medical care or from funeral arrangements). In such cases the right to justice is founded on the dignity of every human being and citizenship and not on sexual activity or orientation.

consecrated celibacy

115. The Church sees great value in the way of life of those who renounce marriage so that they can dedicate themselves to serving the kingdom of God. John the Baptist lived in the wilderness. Jesus had no permanent home of his own. Both remained celibate. The Catholic Church holds that Mary remained a virgin after the birth of Jesus, consecrating her life to her son alone. Paul found freedom in remaining unmarried for the sake of his work as an Apostle. In the third century, Anthony of Egypt heard the call of God to live a radically simple life of prayer in the desert. Later, Basil and Benedict wrote rules of life for religious communities. Monks, nuns and religious congregations of sisters or brothers have preserved the learning of the ancient world, have founded schools and hospitals, have preached the Christian Gospel to the ends of the earth, and have done great works of charity. More fundamentally, by heeding the personal call of God to a life of prayer and simplicity, and by renouncing wealth, family and personal ambition, they have borne witness to the limitations of all earthly goods and been a powerful source of spiritual renewal for the whole Church.

116. For spiritual as well as practical reasons, the Catholic Church in the West also requires priests and bishops to live lives of permanent celibacy, unless they have been given special dispensation. The priests and bishops of the Church, in following the example of Jesus, the good shepherd, seek to give themselves wholeheartedly to the service of the Gospel. Freedom from special family responsibilities allows them to make a greater commitment of time and energy to the demands of their pastoral role. However, the promise of celibacy would be misunderstood if it were seen only in practical terms. Rather, it gains its meaning from the radical character of priestly consecration as the dedication of the whole person to Christ and as a sign of the world that is to come.

the radical character of priestly consecration is a sign of the world that is to come

117. Those who live consecrated lives of celibacy, whether in communities of monks or nuns, in smaller groups of two or three, or as individuals serving a particular local community, live for, with and among other people. To live as a hermit, without human community, is a distinctive vocation to which only a very few are called. In general, the life of consecrated celibacy should involve both a supportive community and the presence of true friendships. Community life, whether in the convent or in the parish, is something like family life: it is not always easy or congenial but at best it involves a real sense of human solidarity. Within this context, true friendship, what St Aelred of Rievaulx called 'spiritual friendship' can exist, both between consecrated celibates and married or single lay people, as well as within religious communities and among fellow priests. Those who have dedicated themselves to God as celibate flourish in their calling through the support of their friends.

the vocation of marriage

118. Married life has great value and importance as a special form of personal relationship. This value is rooted in the nature of man and woman and the covenant partnership of love and common life between them. In those who are blessed with children it receives a still deeper human meaning. Not everyone becomes a parent, but everyone has parents, at least in a biological sense. Parenthood is of immense significance theologically, personally and for society as a whole. These things are true of family and marriage as profound human realities whatever the couple's religious beliefs.

119. For Christians, this deep human reality is given a further level of meaning as a sign and a way of sharing in the love between Christ and his bride, the Church (*Ephesians* 5:22). Catholics see marriage as one of the seven sacraments of the Church, an effective sign of divine love. Marriage is already understood as a gift from God and a fundamental human good, but now it also expresses vocation from God into the life of Christ. When two baptised Christians marry they are joined together by God, and the Holy Spirit is given to them to inspire 'progress towards an ever richer union with each other on all levels - of the body, of the character, of the heart, of the intelligence and will, of the soul' (*The Christian Family in the Modern World,* 1981, paragraph 19). The Sacrament also strengthens those who receive the gift of children so they can welcome them into the life of faith. As marriage reflects the mystery of Christ and the Church the Second Vatican Council called the Christian family 'the domestic Church' (*The Church (Lumen Gentium)* 1964, paragraph 11), a microcosm of the universal Church. The Sacrament of marriage is a reality that endures throughout life as long as both husband and wife remain alive. It creates a bond that cannot be dissolved by any human power.

120. Marriage, then, is a bond, a union or communion, a 'joining together' of a man and a woman. The unitive meaning of married love is something that modern society recognises and aspires to, even if it is not always properly understood. However, problems can be caused by misunderstanding the unitive dimension of sexual love. If it is seen primarily in terms of perfect satisfaction, this cannot but lead to self-doubt, anxiety, disappointment and frustration. It is good for someone to want to please and to be pleased by the one he or she loves, but the conversation of love is endangered if it is reduced to good technique or to the search for some ideally compatible partner. The unitive meaning of sexual love  is best understood not in terms of the perfect experience, but in terms of mutual communication.

121. The secular emphasis on sexual performance as central to the unitive meaning of sexual love has a further negative effect. Concentration on this aspect of a relationship makes it seem only sensible to try out a physical relationship before the public commitment of marriage. Yet, such a provisional context undermines the deeper meaning of marital love, precisely because of the lack of true commitment. It is true that a time of testing and preparation within a relationship before the serious commitment of marriage is vitally important. An idealised image of 'love at first sight' can be misleading and perilous. What is wrong is to see this courtship or engagement as involving sexual intercourse, a 'trial marriage' involving a semblance of commitment without actual commitment.

55

122. In the context of high rates of sexually transmitted diseases and of teenage pregnancies government-sponsored sex education has tended to emphasise the importance of 'safe' or 'safer sex' and has encouraged the use of condoms as the best solution to unwanted pregnancy and the health risks of casual sexual liaisons. However, this approach has been both morally corrosive and practically ineffective - from 1996 to 2002 incidents of the major bacterial sexually transmitted infections more than doubled (*Renewing the focus: HIV and other Sexually Transmitted Infections in the United Kingdom in 2002*, Health Protection Agency). This strategy suffers from the assumption that social and moral problems can be solved in a technical way without addressing questions of behaviour. Sex education should stress the importance of the virtue of chastity, and should promote the value of virginity before marriage and of constancy within marriage. To give instruction on the biology of human reproduction without a principled moral context ignores and obscures what is most specifically human in human sexuality.

human sexuality has both a unitive and procreative dimension

123. Human sexuality has both a unitive and a procreative dimension. The procreation of new human life is the result of sexual union. This is how nearly all children come into existence. If a couple are 'trying for a baby' they make love in the hope of conceiving a child. An unplanned or unexpected pregnancy is sometimes said to be the result of an 'accident', but it is not accidental that a sexual union may result in pregnancy. The sexual union of a man and a woman is 'ordained in itself to the procreating of new life' (*On Human Life (Humanae Vitae)*, 1968 paragraph 11).

124. Marital love, which is the proper human context for sexual intercourse, is likewise related to the good of children. Marriage is more than merely a good context for looking after a child; the desire to have a child with this person is a proper and natural expression of unitive love. Married life is the measure of sexual love and marriage possesses both a unitive and a procreative dimension. These two aspects are not merely biological, but are ordered to something specifically human: a human union and the generation of a human being.

125. It is marital love that is the measure of what is right and chaste in matters of sexual intercourse. The love that is implied by sexual intercourse is exclusive, committed and open to the possibility of new life. This does not mean that the desire for a child is the only acceptable motive for expressing sexual love. Sexual union within marriage can be a moment of celebration, of support, of reconciliation or of a whole range of expressions of married love. Nevertheless, the procreative aspect of sexual love remains an essential part of the human meaning of sexuality, to be respected as such even when the couple is not seeking to have a child. Responsible parenthood will often involve planning when to have children, God willing, but this should not be by means of contraception that places a barrier between the partners, or that suppresses the healthy working of the body to make the act infertile. These actions undermine the full human meaning of sexuality. They also raise other medical and moral questions that should not be overlooked: the long term health implications they may have for women and the serious impact they seem to be having on the environment. In addition to this, some chemical contraceptives do not operate only by preventing conception, but also work by preventing those embryos that are occasionally conceived from implanting.

126. The need for effective family planning requires a different and more radical approach. What is required is reliable knowledge of the cycle of female fertility and a willingness to agree to abstain from sexual union at certain times. The last twenty years have seen great improvements in this area and Natural Family Planning is now regarded by respected medical authorities as being highly effective for those who are instructed by trained teachers and who are strongly motivated. There are also some attractive elements in this approach to family planning. These include self-control, greater awareness of bodily function, the involvement of both partners on an equal basis, and the absence of health risks or dependence on constant use of pharmaceuticals. The values of this holistic and human approach to family planning deserve to be considered seriously.

infertility

127. It is an irony that so many methods of control of fertility exist side by side with the bitter experience of infertility. One in six couples experience difficulties conceiving a child at some time in their lives and this figure appears to be growing. Since 1978 a new technique has been developed to address this problem. *In vitro* fertilisation (IVF) brings the sperm and egg together in the laboratory and the newly conceived human embryo is then transferred into the mother. This has enabled many couples to become parents.

128. Sadly, the technique of IVF also has its darker side. Procreation does not come about as a result of the physical union of the couple in sexual intercourse, but reproduction occurs in the laboratory. The use of fertility drugs and collection of eggs from the woman can have complications. There are often multiple pregnancies, which carry health risks. While healthy and happy children are born, other human embryos are deliberately discarded because they have been judged 'unfit' or 'surplus to requirements'. The ability to screen embryos for genetic characteristics before transferring the ones who are thought desirable has far-reaching consequences. In the future it may be possible for embryos to be selected for sex, physical appearance and other characteristics. Instead of being regarded as a gift, a child would then be treated as a commodity, the product of parental choice. When children are

it is an irony that so many methods of control of fertility exist side by side with the bitter experience of infertility

conceived by a process of production, however sincere the motivation, some form of quality control is very likely to result.

129. The use of donated human gametes in IVF adds further moral complications. If a man donates sperm he becomes an absent blood-father, unacknowledged and perhaps unknown to his child. Present practice involves the falsifying of birth certificates to hide the existence of the known biological father, and the children of donor parents currently have no legal right to search for these parents. The reality of sperm-donor fathers, egg-donor mothers and surrogate mothers threatens to confuse and undermine our sense of biological parenthood and to deprive children of their sense of identity and of their right to know their mothers and fathers. Adoption is not without its problems, but it is the response to a situation that has not been brought about deliberately. The children of donor parents have been deliberately conceived to be estranged from their biological parents. Most chilling of all are the possibilities of cloning a child to be the genetic copy of an existing person, or of conceiving a child whose mother would be a foetus who had been aborted.

130. The heartache of infertile couples should not be ignored. Infertility is a genuine medical problem and treatment and prevention of the causes of infertility is a proper aim of medicine. Infertility frustrates a good and natural human desire - to conceive, bear and rear a child with the person you love, and to whom you are publicly committed. Advances in Natural Family Planning provide some hope in this area, as better knowledge of the cycle of fertility can also be used to increase considerably the likelihood of conception. Further research should not concentrate on techniques that take procreation into the laboratory or that seek ever more control on what sort of child is allowed to be born, but should look into the root causes of infertility and address these directly.

131. Despite advances in medicine, some couples will remain unable to have children. This is something they must ultimately find a way to accept, with the help of God, as they discover what positive destiny

God has in store for them. The love and support which a couple can provide for one another should not be inward looking but can help them to sustain the lives of others in their local community, in their church and in the wider world.

132. Some couples who are childless, and some who already have a family, decide to adopt or foster children. Parents who adopt show true generosity of spirit. However, adoption poses its own problems, especially during adolescence when every young person tends to become more self-conscious and concerned about his or her roots and identity. This process needs to be respected and all adopted children should have the right, if they wish to know, to information concerning their blood relatives. Hopefully, they will come to appreciate that the decision to make a child available for adoption is often a harrowing one and should not be taken to imply a lack of love on the part of their natural (birth) parents. Many such children come through the transition to adulthood very well with good relationships with their families, while for others the pain remains. In cases where things do not seem to have worked out, we should not believe that love was wasted. It may not be possible for us to appreciate the good that has been done. Couples or individuals who adopt deserve appreciation for giving a secure home and a family to children who might otherwise have little hope.

divorce

133. Most people recognise the human need for close, personal and enduring relationships. Nevertheless, divorce has become increasingly common. This is frequently a source of great pain. The divorce proceedings may also add to distress already caused on both sides and the effects on the children may remain through life. The contemporary expectation seems to be that someone who gets divorced should remarry and second marriages are commonly viewed as a positive sign that someone has 'moved on'. The Catholic Church, on the other hand, seeks to follow the teaching of Jesus that marriage is indissoluble: 'What God has united, man must not divide' (*Mark* 10:9).

134. The general claim that divorce is a better option, for the sake of the children, than continuous strife between the parents seems to underestimate the harm that the process of divorce itself involves. Nevertheless, the Church accepts the legitimacy of seeking legal separation in sufficiently serious circumstances. A civil divorce may be needed to give legal and social protection to one or other of the partners that cannot be obtained simply by living separately. Those who divorce normally need help and support and should not be subject to stigma or discrimination. Yet, as civil divorce does not truly dissolve the marriage, the divorced person is not free before God or the Church to marry someone else.

135. Sometimes, after long investigation, the Church will declare that what appeared to be a valid marriage lacked an essential element such that it was not, in fact, a marriage. This is different from a divorce and is called an 'annulment'. If a marriage has broken down irretrievably, a person has the right to have the Church investigate to see if there are grounds for it to be declared null. However, the alleged grounds for nullity may not have been present from the beginning and problems may only have developed later on. In this case an annulment is not possible since the marriage was entered into at the beginning and marriage is indissoluble.

136. The Catholic Church continues to bear witness to the indissolubility of marriage by its sacramental discipline. The Catholic Church in England, Wales, Scotland and Ireland sought to acknowledge the pain caused by this discipline in *One Bread, One Body* (1998). It is important to emphasise that seeking or receiving a divorce, where there are serious and objective reasons for it, is not in itself a barrier to receiving communion. While those who have entered a second relationship after divorce are not permitted to participate fully in the Sacraments, the Church warmly invites and encourages them to become involved in the life and prayer of the local Church community as much as possible.

abuse

137. The Church, in common with all society, condemns the abuse of power and the desire for domination wherever and whenever it is present in the distortion of sexual love. A rapist violates the sexual intimacy of another person and commits an act of great evil which 'wounds the respect, freedom and physical and moral integrity to which every person has a right' (*Catechism of the Catholic Church* (1994), paragraph 2356). Those who have suffered rape often feel unclean or unworthy. The rebuilding of trust and self-confidence is difficult and requires healing. The Church is called to be a place of sanctuary and support for those who have suffered rape.

138. Today, there is greater awareness of domestic violence than in the past, particularly violence directed against women and children, though women and grown-up children can also perpetrate violence against other family members. This greater awareness is a positive development as it is the first step towards addressing a serious moral and social problem. The equal dignity of man and woman is the true basis for a just and fair relationship. Marriage therefore needs to be presented more effectively as a covenant relationship, a partnership of life and love, built on equality and mutual respect.

the equal dignity of man and woman is the true basis for a just and fair relationship

139. In recent years, both society and Church have become more aware of various forms of abuse against children. Children have suffered abuse at home, in the family, in school, in church, and in child-care institutions. Such actions involve a terrible betrayal of trust as they are often committed by the very person entrusted with the child's care. The fact that a number of clergy and religious have been perpetrators of child sexual abuse has caused the Catholic Church profound shame, as well as leading it to review its policies and procedures concerning the protection of children. This mirrors a process that is going on in virtually all institutions and professions that work with children. Following the publication of the Report chaired by Lord Nolan, the Bishops of England and Wales have committed themselves to implement its recommendations. Specifically, the Catholic Office for the Protection of Children and Vulnerable Adults (COPCA) has been set up in order to help make the Church a place of safety and an example of best practice in the protection of children.

140. Child abuse may be physical, sexual, emotional or by neglect. It causes harm that often lasts into adulthood. If the abuser is a parent or if he or she is someone who is supposed to represent God and the Church the harm done can be even greater. Many continue to bear the wounds in their personality, in their close relationships and in their future hopes. Even so, survivors of the various forms of abuse witness to the capacity of the human person to overcome the pain and harm which has been perpetrated. God, who came into the world as a child, can still be found in the process of healing, in those who help in this process and in those who work to protect children.

141. The abuse of children is a worldwide problem. Child molesters make use of the internet to entrap children and sex tourists travel to countries where children can be exploited. Ruthless criminals organise such activity and children may be driven to sell their bodies by extreme poverty. The protection of children from exploitation is an area that requires international cooperation between governments and agencies so that abusers and criminal gangs can be prosecuted and the lives of young people can be improved. The violation of children and young adults, who become slaves of organised prostitution and the sex industry, is a scandalous offence against the dignity of the person. It is important to help those who wish to become free from these situations.

142. Such extreme distortions highlight the need for a teaching and a witness to the positive human meaning of sexuality, especially in regard to the way it can and should unite two persons in mutual love.

support of marriage and the family

143. Marriage and family life need support all the more as the point of marriage is less well appreciated and the basic family unit is more fragile. It therefore seems unwise to grant cohabiting couples the privileges and benefits given to married couples. A couple's unwillingness to declare their commitment publicly must raise some doubt about the level of that commitment. For this reason, the call for the law to treat unmarried couples as though they were married would send a wrong signal to society about the preferred form of family and this in turn could further undermine the stability of marriage, of the family and ultimately of society. As we said in *The Common Good*, 'A well-constructed society will be one that gives priority to the integrity, stability and health of family life' (paragraph 21). At the same time, the human reality of marriage is never simple or tidy. Couples are often all too conscious of the gap between the ideals of marriage and the reality of their daily lives. To encourage married couples, the Bishops' Conference intends to initiate a series of conversations throughout the dioceses of England and Wales to address what it is to live this Sacrament in today's culture.

a well-constructed society will be one that gives priority to the integrity, stability and health of family life

144. Similarly, the diverse forms of family that are becoming more widespread should not be ignored or unfairly disadvantaged. Children now are often brought up by one parent or in a mixed family with children from previous relationships. Wherever and however parents take responsibility, as best they can, for their children's upbringing, they should be affirmed in this. In particular, those who manage on their own and on very limited resources to give children a good upbringing and education deserve all the help they can get. Employers should be flexible so as to attract and keep workers who are lone parents, but governments should not coerce parents with sole responsibility for small children to take up further paid work. Mothers who have chosen the path of life and love by keeping their child deserve financial help from government and practical help from the Church. Volunteers who raise money to help women in these situations are a powerful witness to the Christian way of life.

145. Preparation for marriage is more important now than ever and we affirm the increasing role married lay people are playing in the Church to help in this work. They can help young couples to identify important issues to do with work, money, family relations and children so that these can be faced honestly and talked through. Communication between the couple is central to building up a relationship that is to last them a lifetime. Friends and family can be a great support in encouraging the couple to work at their relationship both when it is going well and at times when it is strained. Counselling services, both those connected with the Church and those with no Christian affiliation, can also be a great help for couples in difficulty. We also appreciate the efforts of those promoting and providing instruction in Natural Family Planning, as such services are often neglected by local general practitioners.

preparation for marriage is more important now than ever

146. Education for sexual integration is an on-going process. Its aim is to nurture the virtue of chastity, that is, of moral maturity in the area of sexual desire. At a young age this is partly a matter for formal education, where parents should be partners with schools in the education of their children. However, what happens in the family home is equally, if not more, important. It is extremely difficult for parents, even when combining with schools and Christian youth groups, to help their children to develop the virtue of chastity, but it is a vitally important task. Key to this process of personal growth is the establishment of self-respect and the ability to form relationships of trust. The many children who do develop to moral maturity and self-possession owe not a little to their relationships with their parents and the example of their parents' relationship with one another.

acting justly

justice, love and humility

147. Acting justly, in the full meaning of this phrase, embraces walking humbly with God, and loving tenderly those around us. It is not only a matter of recognising the equal dignity of all human beings for what they are now, as fellow creatures, but also of seeing in them what God is calling them to be, as fellow heirs of the kingdom of heaven. In the context of the Gospel message, justice is not something that can be established first and then mercy or compassion added afterwards. Rather, it is only the mercy of God that establishes justice and without mercy there can be no justice. This understanding of justice shapes how we judge the imperfect human structures of justice and how we seek to bring about justice in ourselves and in our society.

148. A justice that is founded upon love will seek to be generous hearted and to work especially for those who are in most need. At the same time, it will renounce any kind of injustice or discrimination. The Second Vatican Council stated clearly that 'any kind of social and cultural discrimination in basic personal rights on the grounds of sex, race, colour, social conditions, language or religion, must be curbed and eradicated as incompatible with God's design' (*The Church in the Modern World*, paragraph 29).

149. A justice founded on humility will realise the need to learn from others in order to recognise different forms of injustice and will realise that the justice of the kingdom of God lies in the future and can only be known in part in the present. Acting justly does not imply having a complete knowledge of the future, having a plan of the perfect society or having a scale against which we can weigh all things. It is only God who possesses such knowledge and human claims to possess this kind of perfect knowledge can lead quickly to injustice. Acting justly involves listening, recognising need, avoiding discrimination and working as creatively and as wisely as one can, but also recognising that fruits of justice can only be established by God. 'If the Lord does not build a house, in vain the masons toil' (*Psalm* 127:1).

150. Bodily life is not the only or even the highest good, but it is a basic good and it underpins our existence with each other in the world. Caring for someone's life and health is a way of caring for that person. There are many issues we could have addressed when considering what it is to act justly in the context of cherishing life, but we have chosen to reflect particularly on healthcare, as this has a special place in the service of life and has raised many ethical questions in people's minds. Secondarily we thought it necessary to say something concerning the use of force and especially the use of lethal force in defence of life. These two diverse areas each involve issues of life and death and both are areas of particular contemporary concern. To act justly in cherishing life embraces, among other things, building a society that nurtures the health and that protects the lives of all people from the beginning to the end of life, and one that restrains the attacks of those intent on harming the innocent.

151. In seeking to act justly in regard to healthcare we are immediately confronted by three questions: Who has responsibility for people's health? How should the resources that go into healthcare be shared out? What forms of deliberate harm to life may occur under the guise of caring for health?

responsibility for health

152. The primary responsibility for an adult's health lies with that person. Health is a gift to that person from God and good health is also important in order to fulfil our duties towards others. An adult expresses appreciation for the gift of his or her own health by eating properly, taking sufficient rest and regular exercise, avoiding excessive drinking or smoking, and taking reasonable precautions when driving or doing physical work. It will be necessary to seek medical help promptly when it is needed. Looking after our health is not the only goal in life, and there are circumstances when we may decide to take serious risks with our lives, but most goals are not best promoted by neglecting to take care of our health.

153. It is the responsibility of parents or guardians to care for the health of children and gradually to teach them to take care of themselves. Within the family and among those who live a common life together, the bonds of mutual affection give rise to a proper concern for one another's health. Severe illness can take away our independence and our sense of self-worth, and may also take its toll on the carer who is often a family member. Wider society has a great responsibility to provide financial, emotional and practical support for those who care for a loved one. If the care can be made more sustainable, then not only the sick or disabled person and the carer benefit, but the whole community benefits.

154. Doctors, nurses and other health professionals devote themselves particularly to the goods of life and health. They have a special responsibility for the life and health of any patient who comes to them and whom they can reasonably accept. From its origins, in the days when the Hippocratic oath was written, western medicine has characteristically involved an explicit ethical commitment to proper standards of knowledge, skill and good character. Bodies such as the Royal Colleges were founded to foster this sense of professionalism.

155. The practice of nursing the sick and the institutions of hospitals, hospices and nursing homes have their roots in the ancient virtue of hospitality, taught by all religions. Many congregations of religious sisters and brothers throughout the world follow Jesus by caring for the sick. They have taken nursing care from being something mainly done at home by relatives into a practice that is highly trained and well organised. The example of nursing sisters working in the Crimea had a great effect on Florence Nightingale. Indeed, all nurses, of whatever belief and background, follow a profession that, in its modern form, owes a great deal to these religious congregations.

156. The role of the doctor is to use his or her skill and knowledge for the sake of the life and health of the patient. Where the patient is competent, the primary responsibility for deciding whether treatment should be given or not rests with the patient. Where the patient is incompetent, the doctor should act in the best interests of the patient, taking into account any wishes previously expressed by the patient. Discussion with a doctor about the content of an advance directive may help to clarify options, hopes and wishes with regard to future treatment. Such discussions can be helpful for both doctor and patient.  However, advance directives cannot foresee every circumstance. Furthermore, some forms of advance directive (such as that proposed by the Voluntary Euthanasia Society) have been drawn up deliberately to embody a request for passive euthanasia. We reiterate our judgement that 'the legal enforcement of such directives' is something that should be resisted (A joint submission from the Church of England House of Bishops and the Roman Catholic Bishops' Conference to the House of Lords Select Committee on Medical Ethics (1993), paragraph 19).

157. Health is an important concern not only for the individual and for healthcare professionals, but also for society as a whole. A great deal of ill health is caused by poverty and social injustice. The responsibilities of government and of those groups and individuals within society concerned with public health is expressed first by addressing the general question of living conditions: water, food, housing, sanitation, basic education, employment and social assistance. These factors have a far greater effect on the prevention of illness than does the provision of adequate healthcare.

158. More specifically, however, government also has a role in ensuring that all citizens have access to affordable medical care. The principles of social justice which we set out in *The Common Good* require a proper degree of freedom and independence at the local level but do not require any one particular pattern of ownership or control of healthcare. In different countries some healthcare systems are more centralised and some are more devolved. The combination of public, private and voluntary contribution also varies. (It is important to recognise that organisation and funding are two distinct issues). These national and local variations do not necessarily compromise access, quality or fair distribution of care, but significant structural changes give rise to dangers as well as opportunities. The Church shares the concern of many people that the values of human solidarity, which first inspired the National Health Service, should be maintained through whatever changes may occur in the future. The present difficulties should not blind us to the fact that the NHS has achieved much of great value since its establishment more than fifty years ago.

allocating healthcare resources

159. The issue of resource allocation has a bearing upon many other moral questions. It is easy to say that healthcare funding should be increased, and perhaps there is a case for this, but funding, whether from public or private sources, must have some limit, as it always involves taking money from other deserving causes (for instance: education, social welfare or economic investment for the future). Furthermore, the rising costs of medicine, rising expectations and rising life expectancy make it unlikely that every patient could always immediately receive the most effective treatment irrespective of cost. Some system of rationing seems to be inevitable.

160. It is quite legitimate to distinguish individual cases by seriousness and urgency, but we should be wary of bias that may be built into systems of rationing, especially where this reflects attitudes to whole categories of patient. It is important that scarcity of resources is not used as an excuse for discrimination or even as a justification for inflicting deliberate harm on some patients. Utilitarian calculations to determine who is most deserving of treatment tend to privilege those who are younger and healthier and therefore tend to threaten those who are most in need of help. The

utilitarian calculations tend to threaten those who are most in need of help

explicit or implicit use of age criteria for rationing healthcare 'breaches principles of non-discrimination, equal access to satisfaction of needs, social solidarity and respect for the elderly' (*Healthcare allocation: an ethical framework for public policy*, 2001, page 118).

161. The trust between patient and doctor is an important value which should not be compromised by always making the doctor responsible for the financial decisions about treatment options. Difficult allocation decisions should be made collaboratively by consultation between health service managers and doctors with representation from patients. General parameters should be set out in advance by a process involving the greatest level of participation from different groups within society. There is no simple or technical way to make allocation decisions. They require the virtue of practical wisdom to take into account many different factors and to respect more than one ethical principle at the same time. The aim should be to offer every patient what reasonable hope is available within some system of priority and queuing. The first principle of fair distribution is: 'to each as any has need' (*Acts* 4:35).

medical research, transplantation and gene therapy

162. Scientific research is an essential aspect of modern medicine. Research on animals, especially on higher animals, may involve causing greater suffering than that involved in rearing animals for food. Nevertheless, the Church considers experimentation on animals 'within reasonable limits' to be legitimate if and when 'it contributes to caring for or saving human lives' (*Catechism of the Catholic Church*, paragraph 2417). Experimenting on human subjects is also an important part of medical research, but only with consenting volunteers and only where the risks are reasonable. Experimental procedures which carry an appreciable risk and are not for the subject's benefit should never be conducted on human beings who cannot consent.

163. Surgery is justified when it is for the medical benefit of the person being operated on, or at least does no serious and lasting harm. No one should be mutilated for the sake of healing someone else. However, giving blood or giving bone marrow does no lasting harm and is an admirable way of showing generosity. More risky, and only possible for someone in very good health, is the donation of a kidney or the lobe of a liver. Hospitals in the United Kingdom are right generally to confine such actions to close relatives, so that there is no danger of people being tempted to sell their organs.

Pope John Paul II has praised the 'noble and meritorious' actions of those who freely donate tissues or organs

Pope John Paul II has praised the 'noble and meritorious' actions of those who freely donate tissues or organs.

164. A person is not directly harmed by what is done to his or her body after death. Nevertheless, respectful treatment of human remains is important so as to acknowledge both the memory of the dead and the significance of the human body. The Church has never forbidden the practice of autopsy to discover the cause of death, and has acknowledged the need for doctors to learn from human dissection. In recent years this need, and the need for donors for organ transplant, have been met with great generosity on the part of the public, so that thousands offer their bodies to medicine and millions carry donor cards. However, abuses such as taking organs against the wishes of relatives and without the prior consent of the deceased amount to 'dispossession or plundering of the body' (Pope John Paul II, *Address to the Society for Organ Sharing*, June 1991). Such excesses undermine respect for the human body, and seriously damage public trust. The practice of organ donation will flourish only if it remains a free act of human generosity and, in the case of unpaired vital organs, only if there is certainty that the donor is actually dead.

165. Gene therapy, that is, treating a patient's illness by altering his or her genetic make-up, is still at an early stage but is the focus of much research. Therapy that affects only the patient is called somatic gene therapy. The assessment of somatic gene therapy depends on similar factors that need to be considered in surgery: How safe is this procedure? Is it appropriate for this patient? 'Germ-line' therapy affects the genes of future generations. This raises another set of concerns, associated with eugenics: the attempt to control the genes of a whole society in the mistaken belief that there can and should be perfect human beings. Eugenics has always involved discrimination against people with disabilities. It necessitates an unacceptable level of political control over the type of people who are conceived or who are allowed to be born and it implies a rejection of the idea that children are a gift. Germ-line gene therapy, by making alterations that will be inherited from generation to generation, also itself introduces new and unquantifiable health risks for future generations.

166. Whilst science can show the risks of any development, the moral criterion by which progress is measured is the human person. 'Respect for life, and above all for the dignity of the human person, is the ultimate guiding norm for any sound economic, industrial and scientific progress' (Pope John Paul II *Letter for the World Day of Peace*, 1990).

Not doing harm

167. Acting justly requires not only that we promote good health, but also that we refrain from carelessly inflicting ill health on others. Employers have a duty not to risk injury to workers, or, where this is not possible, at least to minimise the risks and make them known. Negligence which may result in injury is a serious injustice which is made worse by a failure to take responsibility and provide for the victims' healthcare needs.

168. People also risk causing ill health in others if they carry a disease which could be passed on. There is a common duty to take reasonable precautions not to spread infectious diseases such as measles, chicken pox or influenza. In this context, immunising children against infectious diseases is important not only for their sake, but also to protect other children who would otherwise be at more risk of infection. Vaccination has sometimes been controversial because of a real or perceived danger of side-effects, or because the production of certain particular vaccines has involved the use of tissue taken from aborted foetuses. Vaccines sometimes do have side-effects but they also give protection which is important individually and communally. Parents will want to consider the best evidence available and make a prudent decision on how best to protect their child. Some parents may feel called, on reflection, to boycott vaccines that are linked to abortion, so as to bear witness to the injustice of abortion and to the lack of respect shown to the child's remains. Such actions are neither required nor excluded by justice, but are matters of practical wisdom and personal vocation.

169. Complex issues also surround inherited conditions. If someone carries an inherited disease or disability would it not be better to remain childless than deliberately to bring a disabled child into the world? A couple must decide whether they are able to care for such a child. What they should not do is conceive a child with the intention of having it destroyed if it is disabled (whether as an embryo *in vitro*, by abortion, or by deliberate neglect as a new-born baby). Systems of pre-natal diagnosis can involve prejudice against people with disability and undue pressure to screen and to abort. Nevertheless, there are courageous parents who resist the pressure to have pre-natal testing or who refuse to abort a child who has been identified as having some disability. If a couple is able, with help, to tackle the practical difficulties and to give the child the care it needs, then it is not unreasonable for them to try to conceive, even where there is a greater than average risk that the child will inherit a disability. Parents of children with disabilities have testified to the unconditional love they find themselves able to give to such a child and the unifying effect that child has on the rest of the family.

170. Sexually-transmitted diseases also raise difficult issues. Certainly, the risks of passing on (or contracting) such diseases give a further reason why casual sex is irresponsible and contrary to human dignity. If a man or his wife become infected with a serious illness such as HIV, what ways do they have to express their love for one another? The desire to have a child and the sexual expression of love are important values in marriage, but it is important to recognise that the only assured way to prevent passing on such an infection is to express love in ways other than through sexual intercourse. Indeed, this may in fact strengthen and deepen the bond of love between them.

sexually-transmitted diseases give a further reason why casual sex is irresponsible and contrary to human dignity

171. Healthcare professionals are bound to act for the good of their patients, but their role gives them a position of trust which is open to abuse. The patient is vulnerable, both psychologically and physically, and is dependent on the competence and character of those entrusted with the patient's care. Incompetence not only brings the healthcare professions into disrepute, but commits a serious injustice by harming people who are already sick and in need. Careless communication of personal medical information to those not entitled to it can also cause harm both in terms of mental distress and in terms of injury to public reputation. Worse than ignorance or negligence are those exceptional cases where healthcare workers exploit their position of trust and deliberately harm or abuse patients.

172. Medical malpractice and occasional acts of malice by medical personnel are clearly harmful, but a more sinister form of injustice occurs when the very ethos of the healthcare professions starts to be corrupted. This happened with the eugenics movement in the early twentieth century and in particular in Germany in the era of the Nazis, when many doctors and nurses cooperated in enforced sterilisation programmes and in the extermination of disabled and dependent elderly people. The passing of the Abortion Act 1967 has had a corrupting effect on British society as a whole and this has spread to the medical profession, in particular in the area of obstetrics and gynaecology. Many thousands of children a year, while still in their mother's wombs, are being killed, not through incompetence or isolated malice, but because of a corrupting ideology. We fear that there is a real danger that the same pattern may be developing in the treatment of the disabled and the elderly.

abortion

173. Serious reflection on abortion, as on other issues, should start by considering the physical realities of what is done and to whom. The first victim of abortion is the unborn child whose life is ended deliberately. Though it is performed with all the appearances of medical care, and surrounded by euphemisms, termination of pregnancy is the termination of a human life. Taking the life of a child in the womb is as unjust to the unborn child as taking the life of a new born baby is to the infant. The fact that the child is totally dependent on his or her mother, and that the termination is done with the consent of the child's mother, makes it more dreadful, not less. In the words of the Second Vatican Council, both abortion and infanticide are 'abominable crimes' (*The Church in the Modern World*, paragraph 51). For this reason, the law of the Church establishes that a person who actually procures an abortion, fully aware of what they are doing, incurs the penalty of excommunication that can only be rescinded through the Sacrament of reconciliation.

174. Having acknowledged the unborn child, recognition should be given to the difficult circumstances that expectant mothers sometimes find themselves in, and also to the responsibilities of others. The doctor, the father, the employer, the family, the Church and wider society are all involved directly or indirectly in different ways and each has responsibilities. There may be financial or other pressures, and those around the expectant mother may fail to give her the support she needs and deserves. A boyfriend, parent or friend may even try to push her into terminating the pregnancy. 'Sometimes the woman is subjected to such strong pressure that she feels psychologically forced to have an abortion.' (*The Gospel of Life*, paragraph 59) In such cases the woman would be much less blameworthy for her decision.

175. In a secondary sense, the woman is also a victim for she loses her child, but is unable to grieve effectively. The Church 'does not doubt that in many cases it was a painful and even a shattering decision. The wound in your heart may not yet have healed.' (*The Gospel of Life*, paragraph 99) There are other people who share the blame for what happened, but it is the woman herself who must live with the consequences. Post-abortion trauma is common and in some cases severe, though those who feel guilt and remorse are in a healthier state than those who never allow themselves to grieve or to feel guilty. The Church wishes to protect the lives of unborn children and also to support expectant mothers so they do not feel forced to make such a harmful choice. The Church welcomes women who feel remorse over an abortion and who come

the Church wishes to protect the lives of unborn children and also to support expectant mothers

seeking forgiveness, reconciliation and absolution. As a result of such experiences some have been able to become 'among the most eloquent defenders' of everyone's right to life.

176. There is an important distinction to be made between abortion, in which a living human being is destroyed, and contraception, in which no human being is conceived: 'contraception and abortion are specifically different.' (*The Gospel of Life*, paragraph 13) They are, however, closely connected, 'as fruits of the same tree'. This distinction is clear in the case of barrier methods, but it has become blurred by forms of so-called contraception which work in part by preventing the embryo from implanting in the womb and which, in moral terms, are abortifacients. The 'morning after pill' relies primarily on this effect. People of good will should do whatever they can to avoid killing the innocent, and should therefore avoid using or selling drugs that work by destroying human beings once they have been conceived. They should also demand that pharmaceutical companies be honest and explicit in saying how their drugs achieve their effects so that the public can make properly informed decisions.

embryo experimentation

177. *In vitro* fertilisation raises issues about procreation and parenthood, but it also raises concerns about society's attitudes to the lives of those embryonic human beings it creates. While in principle every embryo conceived in the laboratory could be transferred to its mother, in practice of the many conceived only a proportion are given the chance of life. Most are discarded or frozen, perhaps to be transferred later, perhaps only to be discarded or used in experiments. This is a great injustice. Even worse is the practice of conceiving human embryos for the sole purpose of scientific experimentation.

178. Cloning is the deliberate production of genetically identical offspring. Scientists have now succeeded in cloning some animals, the most famous being Dolly the sheep. However, in the case of Dolly, hundreds of embryos had to be cloned before a reasonable number of pregnancies could be achieved, and there were many miscarriages and lambs born with abnormalities before one healthy lamb was born. Even that one apparently healthy lamb, Dolly, subsequently developed premature arthritis. If something similar was attempted in human beings the most likely results would be miscarriage, stillbirth and children born with severe disabilities. The human cost would be enormous and for no good reason. Even if it became safe, the surviving cloned babies would be deprived of a genetic mother and father and would live in the shadow of their genetic original. They would be objects of manipulation that had been produced to a pre-existent specification and would not have been received as a gift as children deserve to be. This would be invidious and unjust.

medical research which involves the destruction of human embryos is a crime against their dignity as human beings

179. It has recently been suggested that cloned human embryos could be used as a source of stem cells which could be useful in future medical advances. This is usually termed 'therapeutic cloning', though it would not be therapeutic for the cloned embryos who would be destroyed for their cells. The process is also euphemistically called 'cell nuclear transfer': a title which disguises the fact that the aim is to produce human embryos and then make use of them. Therapeutic cloning would be far worse than full pregnancy cloning as it would set up a system in which human embryos were cloned only to be destroyed so that their cells could be 'harvested'. Medical research which involves the destruction of human embryos is 'a crime against their dignity as human beings' (*The Gospel of Life*, paragraph 63). It should also be noted that there are good alternative sources of stem cells which do not require cloning or the destruction of embryos. Stem cells taken directly from adults are already being used in medicine and appear to represent the most promising way forward for stem cell therapy.

suicide and euthanasia

180. Human life is under threat in our contemporary society both at the beginning and at the end of life. This can be seen in shifting attitudes to suicide and euthanasia. Suicide is a deliberate act or omission by which a person aims to bring about his or her own death. Such self-destructive action contradicts the proper love of life. It is also a form of rejection or abandonment of family and society. It is hard to live if we feel that we are a burden to others, but suicide leaves those left behind with a far greater burden. To add to their grief, in many cases they feel that they have been unable to help and that they failed to provide sufficient reason for the loved one to go on living. Suicide is the ultimate inability to accept the gift of life.

181. Suicide should never be romanticised, promoted or encouraged. On the other hand, attempting suicide is typically the act of a desperate person and it should be greeted with compassion rather than with blame. It is for this reason that the Suicide Act 1961 decriminalised suicide. The aim of the new law was not to encourage suicide and assisting suicide remained a serious crime. Suicide was thought of as a terrible act, but the help that suicidal people needed was seen as more easily given if those who survived the attempt were not treated like criminals. Most of all, those who contemplate ending their lives need to be given a sense of hope in life.

182. The Church is increasingly aware of the pressures that bring people to attempt suicide and which reduce the moral culpability of their actions. Therefore, the Church publicly expresses hope for their eternal salvation. 'We should not despair of the eternal salvation of persons who have taken their own lives. By ways known to him alone, God can provide the opportunity for salutary repentance. The Church prays for persons who have taken their own lives.' (*Catechism of the Catholic Church*, paragraph 2283)

183. In recent years voices have been heard in favour of legalising euthanasia and assisted suicide. Sometimes it is said that people have a right to 'die with dignity', by which is meant, a right to be killed on request. Euthanasia is worse than suicide, for it involves the intentional killing of someone else, albeit someone who may have asked to be killed. Those who take someone else's life take to themselves the power of life and death and decide that another person's life is without value. If someone is suicidal, pushing him or her over the brink is not helping, it is harming. This is obvious when young and healthy people attempt suicide. Since, however, elderly, sick and disabled people may succumb more easily to doubts about the worth or value of their continued existence, it is even more important to affirm the inherent dignity of their lives.

> *those who take someone else's life decide that another person's life is without value*

184. Respecting the dignity of people who are dying must involve respecting their lives, for without life there is no dignity. Furthermore, legalising euthanasia represents a grave danger for many vulnerable people. This was clearly recognised by the House of Lords Select Committee on Medical Ethics which reported in 1994. Having heard the arguments for legalisation at length, it unanimously concluded that legalising voluntary euthanasia would be wrong in principle and dangerous in practice, not least for the vulnerable. What is needed most of all is adequate support for those who need long term care and for the disabled. Greater knowledge of palliative medicine within the medical profession and an expansion of the work of the hospice movement are also essential, so that those who are near death can be confident of proper care and respect right up until the end.

185. There is a basic level of nursing care that is demanded by human solidarity. We all recognise that leaving a patient cold, unclean, in pain or without human contact for significant periods of time would fall below a decent standard of care. Within the health service, great efforts are made to maintain high standards in this area, despite the pressure of resources and limited staff. In general, providing food and fluids should also be considered basic care. However, when patients are in the final phase of dying they should not be troubled by intrusive treatment and efforts to place or replace a feeding tube may well be excessive or burdensome. What is not morally acceptable is to withdraw tube-feeding, or other life-sustaining treatment, precisely in order to end a patient's life. This would cross the line from reasonable withdrawal of inappropriate treatment into the realm of passive euthanasia.

186. As life is given by God, so we should be ready to meet God in death when the time comes. For Christians this is a time in which fear and sadness are mixed with hope and love. It is an occasion to surrender ourselves into the hands of God. It is wrong for us to anticipate God's command and bring about our own deaths, but one may forgo excessively burdensome treatment. In 1980 the Congregation for the Doctrine of the Faith produced a clear statement concerning these questions: *A Declaration on Euthanasia*.

187. It is important to emphasise that the alleviation of pain is a worthy aim even when the treatment itself carries the risk of shortening life. In such cases there need be no intention of seeking death. It should also be noted that high doses of painkillers do not shorten life in all cases. If the dose is increased gradually over some time the patient will develop a level of tolerance. Nevertheless, in cases where it is foreseen that high doses of painkillers will shorten someone's life, it may still be reasonable to use them to counter the pain. The Church's *Declaration on Euthanasia* is clear: 'In this case, of course, death is in no way intended or sought, even if the risk of it is reasonably taken; the intention is simply to relieve pain effectively.' On the other hand, what is not acceptable is the deliberate use of painkillers as a means to euthanasia.

the use of force

188. Medicine is directed towards cherishing life by caring for those who are sick or in danger of death. A quite different human activity directed to the care and protection of life is the work of the police force and a criminal justice system. In every society there are people willing to resort to violence to achieve their own ends, people who threaten the lives and well-being of others. The state exists for the sake of its citizens, to ensure that they can live in peace with freedom and security. To accomplish this it is sometimes necessary to oppose force with force. Thus the state authorises certain people, under certain conditions, to restrain or resist those who attack the common good or who resort to violence. People talk of 'law and order', and disorder can certainly be a cause of harm and injustice, but the fundamental aim of policing ought not to be the imposition of order but the promotion of justice by protecting the public from unjust attack.

every human life, from conception to death, deserves the full protection of the law

189. The growth of organised crime associated with drugs and the rise of gun culture has made the work of the police increasingly difficult. It becomes necessary in certain circumstances to bear arms and to use lethal force. Recognising that the use of lethal force is legitimate as a last resort, we share the concerns of those people who are deeply uneasy about the increasing use of arms by the police. We encourage the police to continue to look for alternatives to the use of lethal force for restraining dangerous individuals.

190. Those who commit themselves to protecting the security of the nation's citizens as members of the police have a great responsibility and perform an important service to the community. To improve the trust of the people, there must be good relations and open channels of communication between the police and all sections of the local community. The local community need to support the police in their work and the police must be seen to be accountable for their actions. It is essential to the establishment of justice that everyone within a jurisdiction is treated as equal before the law. It is equally important that laws themselves are just and do not unfairly discriminate against any group or individuals. Not every injustice should be illegal, but the law of the land should certainly protect all human beings, however young or old, from deliberate actions causing death or serious injury. In this respect, every human life, from conception to death, deserves the full protection of the law.

191. The Church teaches that one may defend one's own life, or the life of another, even if one foresees that the aggressor may be seriously harmed or may even be killed. The primary purpose of such defence is the preservation of life. However, to use more than necessary force is unjust. The boundary between legitimate and illegitimate force is sometimes difficult to identify but the use of lethal force by private citizens should be even more tightly circumscribed than the use of such force by the police.

192. The strong emotions of hurt and pain felt by the victims of crime, especially as these are reported by the media, can lead to calls for retribution and revenge. After recent particularly horrific violent crimes, there have been outbreaks of vigilantism. Though these feelings can be understood, it is the task of the police and the courts, not of private individuals, to bring to account those suspected of crime. We must also maintain the vital distinction between those we must assume to be innocent and those who have been proven guilty and ensure that each person is treated with justice and has the right to a fair trial. It is for this reason that we caution against any erosion of the double jeopardy rule by which someone cannot be tried for the same crime twice. In a second trial it would be very difficult for any jury to begin with a presumption of innocence.

193. For Christians the right of the State to punish offenders with imprisonment is governed by the requirements that the punishment be just, reasonable and likely to be effective. Prison sentences should reflect the gravity of the crime. A sentence is effective if it establishes justice and facilitates rehabilitation. Pope John Paul II has written, 'In this way authority also fulfils the purpose of defending public order and ensuring people's safety, while at the same time offering the offender an incentive and help to change his or her behaviour and be rehabilitated' (*The Gospel of Life*, paragraph 56). A system of justice should generally aim to integrate the criminal back into society, whenever this is possible without further endangering other members of society. Since the exhortation of the Gospel is to be reconciled with one's brother or sister, a Christian response should never be 'Lock them up and throw away the key.' We encourage courts and governments to explore further forms of restorative justice in which criminals face the results of their crimes with the aim of facilitating recognition of what they have done and reconciliation.

194. Accepting the need to maintain peace in society, the Church has allowed the possibility that capital punishment may be used as a last resort in extreme situations. However, Pope John Paul II has stated that 'as a result of steady improvements in the organisation of the penal system, such cases are very rare, if not practically non-existent.' (*ibid.*) This statement of the Pope is exceedingly strict and shows a development of the Church's practical judgement on this matter. We welcome the fact that the United Kingdom has completely abolished the death penalty and made an international commitment to its permanent abolition by ratifying Protocol 6 of the *European Convention on Human Rights*. The abolition of capital punishment bears witness to the sanctity of life and helps a society to become more consistent in cherishing every human life.

the abolition of capital punishment bears witness to the sanctity of life

war and peace

195. War always involves the use of lethal force and results in the loss of life, not only of soldiers, but also of innocent civilians. The destruction to homes, crops and infrastructure and the presence of landmines and unexploded munitions also causes great hardship even after the war is over. All wars bring great evils, few wars bring great benefits. Nevertheless, for most of Christian history the Church has accepted the argument that unjust aggression should be resisted by legitimate political authorities so that these authorities can defend the common good and protect innocent life. Such resistance requires the use of force up to and including lethal force. While encouraging the work of peace and the building of competent international authorities to prevent warfare, the Catholic Bishops of the Second Vatican Council acknowledged that governments possess a right to lawful self-defence. (*The Church in the Modern World*, paragraph 79) This teaching follows the Christian tradition of just war theory, the aim of which is to limit the outbreak of war and to govern the way in which war may be waged.

196. According to just war theory, the war must have a just cause. The only legitimate reason for waging war is to oppose a great evil that cannot effectively be opposed by any other means. It should always be an act of self-defence and not an act of aggression. The decision to go to war should be taken as a last resort after all other political, economic and diplomatic means have been exhausted. It must be waged by a legitimate ruler and, where this exists, be authorised by international law or mandate. It ought also to reflect a fair degree of popular support. It must have a reasonable prospect of success in military terms and be confident of achieving its objective without causing more harm than the evil it opposes. Finally, the intentions of those who fight the war must be upright: acting for the sake of the stated cause and not for the sake of strategic or economic gain, empire or conquest. There must also be an intention to use only legitimate means, for instance, discriminating between the combatants and non-combatants, not targeting the population as a whole and not using weapons of mass destruction.

197. What has never been accepted by the Church is usurping God's authority over life and death by deliberately killing those who are not engaged in unjust aggression. The killing of unarmed prisoners of war, indiscriminate bombing, the use of weapons of mass destruction, and the targeting of schools, hospitals or residential areas cannot be regarded as legitimate military tactics. Even if these were done in a good cause, they would not be acts of war but acts of terror.

198. Although war may sometimes be just, it is a scandal that throughout the world so much money is spent on armaments while so little is spent addressing poverty. Furthermore, the proliferation and accumulation of all these weapons makes the world a less secure and more dangerous place. According to the Second Vatican Council the arms race is 'one of the greatest curses on the human race and the harm it inflicts on the poor is more than can be endured' (*The Church in the Modern World*, paragraph 81). Public authorities have a duty to regulate the arms trade because the production and the sale of arms has such a great effect on the common good of the international community. The aim of regulation should be to prevent those intent on aggression from acquiring weapons and to prevent commercial interests becoming prejudicial to international peace and security.

199. As we have previously written, 'The Catholic Church has long proclaimed the need to ban nuclear weapons.' (Statements from the November 1997 and 1998 Bishops' Meetings). The Holy See has welcomed the *United Nations Millennium Summit Declaration* which resolved 'to strive for the elimination of weapons of mass destruction, particularly nuclear weapons.' Following the lead taken by the Holy See at the United Nations, we urge the government further to develop and implement the policy of eradicating nuclear weapons including, of course, its own arsenal as well as the weapons of other nations.

the Church has a special role in speaking out against terrorism

200. The Church has a special role in speaking out against terrorism. It can never be just or right to kill and maim innocent civilians as a means of putting pressure on a government or of demoralising a community, even when that government or community is itself acting unjustly. Terrorism also strengthens the hand of oppressive governments and damages the cause of those who resort to it. It often breeds a cycle of violence between neighbouring peoples and poisons the possibility of just and peaceful coexistence. Nevertheless, a proper response to terrorism must be based on justice and law, not on vengeance. It is important that the present rhetoric of a 'war against terror' does not take away from the search for long-term political solutions to conflict, through commitment to justice and negotiation.

201. While legal remedies may establish order, peace in society requires justice, which leads to reconciliation and healing. Peace is also the fruit of love and mercy which are prerequisites for justice in the full meaning of that term. To build a peaceful society, it is necessary to overcome gross economic, social and political inequalities in the world. Peace is threatened when governments or dictators are concerned with building a military arsenal rather than meeting the basic needs of their people. Overcoming war demands establishing a just international order and building up of a culture in which life is cherished.

the culture of life

responsibilities of society

202. As human beings each of us has a common responsibility to help build a culture that upholds the worth of every human life, especially that of the most vulnerable. This common responsibility involves different specific responsibilities at different levels: international, national, local and individual. National and international issues, such as global peace, international trade and climate change, require action at a higher level, by the enactment of laws and treaties and by effective cooperation between governments.

203. Today, more than ever before, governments are responding to their people's demands for global action to protect human dignity. Such responses include proposals to cancel debt in developing countries, to pursue ethical trade and investment policies and to safeguard the environment. The resources of the world require prudent stewardship, while the unequal distribution of natural, technical and educational resources traps whole nations in poverty. Businesses now exist across national boundaries and exercise great political and economic power yet without being wholly accountable to any one national government. Such problems cannot be tackled by any one country acting alone, but only cooperatively.

204. The United Nations as an organisation represents the noble ideal of bringing nations into constructive cooperation for the good of the whole of humanity, and is an important forum to facilitate cooperative action in the search for international peace. Through various peacekeeping interventions and humanitarian initiatives, it has brought justice and hope to many situations of tragedy and disaster. In this way it has been a positive agent for promoting a culture of life. However, as a body it cannot create human rights and values, but must always work in accordance with them. It would seem that some UN initiatives have consistently undermined an authentic vision of human dignity by imposing population control programmes upon developing nations including promotion of abortion and sterilisation.

205. Similarly, the European Union has been a powerful force for peace, cooperation and understanding between its member states, and has the capacity to express and deepen a shared consensus on human dignity and rights. However, it remains true that the European Court of Justice, for example, has sometimes interpreted human rights in a way that would erode the status of marriage and the family as the basic unit of society. The fact that the court's decisions are not subject to scrutiny or correction by elected representatives is a further cause for concern. It is important that conscientious people within the European legal system work to review past judgements and to prevent future judgements that would be harmful to the common good, to authentic human flourishing and to the sanctity of life. (*The Common Good*, paragraphs 99-101)

206. In the United Kingdom it is elected representatives who enact laws and institute public policies. The mandate to govern is derived from the will of the people, but members of parliament should not always act according to what is most popular at any particular time. Those who are in government should exercise power in a principled way. They have a duty to serve the true values of society, the family, and the person, in the context of the common good. Sometimes they fail to do this and instead enact unjust laws that have a harmful effect on society. The recent decision to permit the cloning of human embryos for use in medical research is an example of a law that fails to protect human life and that allows human beings to be used as a means to an end. It is legal but it is not moral.

those who are in government have a duty to serve the true value of society, the family, and the person, in the context of the common good

207. Pope John Paul II has stressed that the purpose of law is to uphold the fundamental rights that belong innately to every human person. Human rights are not created by democracy but are rooted in intrinsic human and moral values. They 'flow from the very truth of the human being' (*The Gospel of Life*, paragraph 71). The Catholic moral tradition has consistently upheld the need for laws to be informed by human moral values if they are to be legitimate and morally binding. Parliamentarians should work towards the abolition of immoral laws. However, sometimes it is impossible to achieve the complete abolition of a bad law. In this situation, it may be permissible to support attempts to reduce the harmful effects of a particular piece of legislation. This is a matter for careful judgement because attempting to reach a compromise may result in passing a law that is harmful in some new way. Legislators should not cooperate in the creation of a worse evil in their efforts to avert an established evil.

208. The rights of some people, for example, the unborn, the disabled, the terminally ill, the homeless and asylum seekers are so fragile that they demand uncompromising protection to ensure justice. As *The Common Good* states: 'The test of every institution or policy is whether it enhances or threatens human dignity and indeed human life itself.' (*The Common Good*, paragraph 13).

responsibilities of citizens

209. The responsibilities people have depend on the roles they occupy within various interlinked communities. A government minister will have responsibilities that go with that office, but will also occupy many other roles, for instance, as a son or daughter, a parent, friend, neighbour, local resident, the trustee of a small charity or the governor of a local school. Sometimes people withdraw from a role or lose a position, sometimes people have responsibility thrust upon them. Our duties are not fixed but depend on our situation.

210. Most people contribute as citizens to building a culture of life through their work and voluntary work, through local political activity, and through self-education and shared discussion. Those who work in healthcare, in education or in social work are able to help others in a very direct way. Others give their time and energy freely to help in practical ways, volunteering to work in a drop-in centre for the homeless or at a hospice, at a refuge for those who have been affected by domestic violence or at a house offering a practical alternative for those facing pressure to have an abortion. Those who cannot work in these areas can support this work by prayer and financial assistance. For each person there are ways of helping to cherish life.

for each person there are ways of helping to cherish life

211. An important place in building up a culture of life goes to families. The commitment to a common life of love is at the heart of living truthfully. It is here especially that we see the care and education of children, the care of those who are sick or disabled and the care of the elderly. These practices bear witness both to the value of life and to the power of love. The love and support that exist within family relationships makes great achievements possible. Governments and voluntary agencies can complement and support but cannot replace this type of care.

212. When faced with a general election, every voter has a responsibility to act for the common good. Whatever may have been the case in the past, representatives to our legislative bodies are now almost always chosen on the basis of a party manifesto, and it is reasonable that people should pay as much attention to the party as to the person. In deciding which party to vote for, the voter needs to consider as wide a spectrum as possible of the policies proposed in the manifesto. Voting in a general election should seldom if ever be based on a single issue, because elections are concerned with a whole range of issues very many of which are concerned with life and with human flourishing. 'A general election must never be confused with a single-issue referendum.' (*The Common Good*, paragraph 65)

213. Nevertheless, in considering the views of the particular candidate, account must be taken of their attitude to the most vulnerable. We recommend that voters ask candidates about their voting intentions on a range of issues, giving priority to issues where innocent lives are at risk. Voters should also discover how their representative in Parliament or in the Welsh Assembly has voted on these issues. As we said in *The Common Good*, 'The attitude of a candidate on that one issue may indicate a general philosophy or personal bias, for instance, contempt for those who uphold the sacredness of human life, which Catholics (and many others) will find deeply objectionable' (*The Common Good*, paragraph 64).

214. Our political responsibilities as citizens are not limited to how we use our vote. On important matters we can also express our concern by writing to or seeing our MP. We could become involved in discussion through the local media or the internet. We might join with others to campaign or, on occasion, demonstrate publicly. We should seek to become better informed on difficult issues to gain some clarity for ourselves and so that we can make more of a contribution in our dialogue with others.

responsibilities of the church

215. The Church is both a spiritual communion, whose members are bound together by their faith and love as disciples of Jesus Christ, and a visible institution, a worldwide body with an organisational framework of law and practice, of bishops, dioceses, schools and parishes. It has the characteristics of both an extended spiritual family and of a highly organised society, and these are mutually supportive. (*The Church* paragraphs 8, 12)

216. The actions of individual Christians who are working in society to build a culture in which life is cherished must therefore be understood as actions of the Church. All that has been said of the responsibilities of legislators and citizens certainly applies to Christians who find themselves in these roles. The Church should not be identified only with its public structures and its teaching mission, but must include all the lay faithful and all that is done out of faith in Christ. At the same time, the public teaching of the bishops and the work that goes on in the context of parishes, Church schools and hospitals and Christian voluntary organisations is also important. Things that are done in a visibly Christian context both achieve a great deal in themselves and also bear witness to the Gospel's message of life and in this way help to support and inspire those who are working for the same end in more secular contexts.

217. As Jesus was sent by God, so he sent out his followers to bring the message of life to all the peoples of the world. While all members of the Church are charged to proclaim the Christian way of life by living it, the bishops have a particular mandate deriving from Christ's instruction to his apostles: 'Go, therefore, make disciples of all nations... and teach them to observe all the commands I gave you' (*Matthew* 28:19-20).

218. The Catholic moral tradition's message of justice and respect for human dignity is more effectively proclaimed and heard when the Church itself, as an institution, seeks to practice what it preaches. As the 1971 bishops' synod document recognised: 'anyone who ventures to speak to people about justice must first be just in their eyes' (*Justice in the World*, paragraphs 40-48). This has various practical implications for establishing and maintaining right relationships for all those living and working within the Church.

219. *Cherishing Life* is a teaching document of the Roman Catholic Bishops of England and Wales. It aims not only to help practising Catholics but also to support all men and women of good will who seek to cherish human life, and especially those who work for the most vulnerable. There is here a message for society, a message for all citizens, and a message that the Church also needs to heed: To seek justice for every human life we need to learn what it is to walk humbly and to love tenderly. If we seek to solve the problems of justice in abstraction from the context of humility and love then we will fail both to understand justice and to bring about the justice we seek. 'This is what the Lord asks of you: only this, to act justly, to love tenderly and to walk humbly with your God.' (*Micah* 6:8)

bibliography of church documents

Scriptural references are from the Jerusalem Bible

The following are Church documents referred to in Cherishing Life, arranged chronologically. It should be noted that some are more authoritative than others.

Council of Trent: *Decree on Justification*

Second Vatican Council: *The Church* (*Lumen Gentium*) (1964)

Second Vatican Council: *The Church in the Modern World* (*Gaudium et Spes*) (1965)

Second Vatican Council: *On the Relation of the Church to Non-Christian Religions* (*Nostra Aetate*) (1965)

Pope Paul VI: *On Human Life* (*Humanae Vitae*) (1968)

Bishops' Synod: *Justice in the World* (1971)

Congregation for the Doctrine of the Faith: *Declaration on Euthanasia* (1980)

Catholic Bishops' Conference of England and Wales: *Abortion and the Right to Life* (1980)

Pope John Paul II: *The Christian Family in the Modern World* (*Familiaris Consortio*) (1981)

Pope John Paul II: *Letter for the World Day of Peace* (1990)

Pope John Paul II: *Address to the Society for Organ Sharing* (1991)

Catholic Bishops' Conference of England and Wales together with Bishops of the Anglican Church: *A joint submission from the Church of England House of Bishops and the Roman Catholic Bishops' Conference of England and Wales to the House of Lords Select Committee on Medical Ethics* (1993)

Pope John Paul II: *The Splendour of Truth* (*Veritatis Splendor*) (1993)

Anglican-Roman Catholic International Commission: *Life in Christ* (1994)

Pope John Paul II: The Gospel of Life (*Evangelium Vitae*) (1995)

Catholic Bishops' Conference of England and Wales: *The Common Good and the Catholic Church's social teaching* (1996)

Approved by Pope John Paul II: *Catechism of the Catholic Church* (1997)

Cardinal Hume: *A Note Concerning the Teaching of the Catholic Church Concerning Homosexual People* (1997)

Catholic Bishops' Conference of England and Wales: *Statement on elimination of nuclear weapons* (1997) in Briefing December 1997 (see http://www.catholicchurch.org.uk/briefing/9712/9712004.htm) and 1998 (see http://www.catholicchurch.org.uk/CN/98/981120b.htm)

Catholic Bishops' Conference of England and Wales: *Human Rights and the Catholic Church* (1998)

Catholic Bishops' Conference of England and Wales together with Catholic Bishops' Conference for Scotland and Catholic Bishops' Conference for Ireland: *One Bread, One Body* (1998)

Pope John Paul II: *Address to the Transplantation Society* (2000)

Prepared on behalf of The Catholic Bishops' Joint Bioethics Committee: *Healthcare Allocation: An Ethical Framework for Public Policy* (2001)

Catholic Bishops' Conference of England and Wales: *The Call of Creation: God's Invitation and the Human Response* (2002)

Catholic Bishops' Conference of England and Wales together with the Bishops' Conference of Scotland in association with CAFOD and SCIAF: *Trade and Solidarity* (2003) published in Briefing vol 33 issue 7 July 2003 p17, available online at www.catholicchurch.org.uk/CN/030530.htm

index

numbers refer to paragraph numbers